Land Revenue Administration in India

Land Revenue Administration in India

S. C. RAY, M. A.

GYAN

Published by

Gyan Publishing House
5, Ansari Road
Daryaganj, New Delhi-110002
Phone: 011-47034999, 9811692060
E-mail: books@gyanbooks.com

Distribution Network
gyanbooks.com
India, USA, Canada, UK, Australia, France

ISBN: 978-81-212-8732-6 (PB)
First Published, 1915

2nd Impression 2023

Printed at: Gyan Press, Delhi.

Land Revenue Administration in India
Author: S. C. Ray

Land Revenue Administration in India

CALCUTTA UNIVERSITY

Land Revenue Administration in India

(*PRESCRIBED FOR THE B.A. EXAMINATION*)

COMPILED BY

S. C. RAY, M.A.

ASST. PROFESSOR OF ECONOMICS

Published by the

CALCUTTA UNIVERSITY

1915

Table of Contents

INTRODUCTION.

PAGES.

THE UNITED PROVINCES.

INTRODUCTION.

The want of a book on Land Revenue administration in India suitable for the B. A. Examination of this and other Indian Universities has long been felt by teachers and students. Nearly twelve months ago, the Board of Studies in Economics, at my suggestion, recommended to the Syndicate the publication by this University of such a book. Owing, however, to the want of detailed technical knowledge of the subject on the part of those likely to undertake the work, it was decided to publish selections from official reports and to adapt them to the requirements of the students. Selections were accordingly made from the red-letter reports of the five major provinces and circulated to the local governments for favour of revision. They have readily and cheerfully responded to our request, and two of them, in particular, viz, the United Provinces and Bombay governments have, with commendable alacrity and generosity, entirely re-written the chapters submitted to them for revision. The University is under profound and grateful obligation to those officers of the local governments who have taken such warm and practical interest in the work with a view to ensure its usefulness. The first chapter, which has been taken from the recent Decennial Report on the Moral and Material Progress of India, purports to be a general introduction to the whole subject, which is dealt with in detail in the subsequent chapters. The book can, therefore, claim to be an authoritative compilation on Land Revenue administration and can safely be placed in the hands of all University students of economics. The University of Calcutta has adopted it as a text-book for the B.A. Examination, and it is hoped that other Indian Universities will find it suitable for their students.

DARBHANGA BUILDINGS,
April 15, 1915.

S. C. RAY.

Land Revenue Administration in India.

INTRODUCTORY.

I.—Land Revenue and Tenures.

Extracts from the Report on the Moral and Material Progress of India, Decennial Issue, 1913, pp. 170-74.

The Land Revenue system and the laws regarding land tenures are matters of immediate interest to a great majority of the population of India, and the most important branch of administration in every province is that connected with the assessment and collection of land revenue, and with the numerous subsidiary questions arising in regard to land. In spite of the gradual development of other forms of industry, agriculture continues to hold by far the most important place, and a large proportion of workers on the land either own or lease the land that they work. Apart, therefore, from its purely financial aspect the Land Revenue and its administration are of great importance from the social and political point of view.

The land revenue of modern India is a form of public income derived from the immemorial custom of the country. In its primary shape it was that portion of the cultivator's grain-heap that the State annexed for the public use, and this crude method of realising the bulk of the State income appears to have been practically the only method in force throughout the greater part of India until the sixteenth century. Revenue is indeed still levied in this manner in many of the native states, and there are large tracts where rents are so taken by landlords. Under the Moghal rule, cash payments—fixed, when possible, for a period of years—were to a large extent substituted for payment in kind, but under later rulers the collection of land revenue became practically little more than a disorganised scramble for the greatest amount of income that could be wrung from the land. As the several provinces came under British control, their assessments were gradually reduced to order, the systems selected being at first tentatively adopted according to the varying circumstances of the different tracts, and becoming more and more crystallised as time went on.

Zamindari and Ryotwari Tenures.—A number of different systems were thus evolved on lines that were for the most part mutually independent. It is usual to differentiate them roughly on broad lines according to the status of the person from whom the revenue is actually demanded. When the revenue is assessed on an individual or community owning an estate, and occupying a position identical with, or analogous to, that of a landlord, the assessment is known as *Zamindari*; when the revenue is assessed on individuals who are the actual occupants, or are accepted as representing the actual occupants, of smaller holdings, the assessment is known as *Ryotwari*. The distinction has its historic origin in the varying degrees in which, in different parts of the country, tribal occupation of territory had superseded the rights of the ruler, or full proprietary rights had been granted to the individual. Under *zamindari* tenure the land is held as independent property, under *ryotwari* tenure it is held of the Crown in a right of occupancy, which is, however, under British rule, both heritable and transferable. Under either system there may be rent-paying sub-tenants. The *Zamindari*, or landlord, system prevails in Bengal, the United Provinces, the Punjab (proprietary cultivating communities), and the Central Provinces—over rather more than half of British India altogether—and the *Ryotwari*, or peasant proprietary system in Bombay, Madras, Assam and Burma. In the Punjab and the United Provinces the present tendency is for co-sharers to divide their responsibilities and become directly responsible to Government for their separate shares.

Permanent and Temporary Settlements.—A second general distinction is that between the areas in which the assessment is permanently fixed and those in which it is fixed for a period of years only. In 1793 the assessment in Bengal was declared to be fixed in perpetuity, and the settlement then made, with some subsequent additions, constitutes what is known as the Permanent Settlement of Bengal. Shortly afterwards the permanent system was extended to the Benares districts (now in the United Provinces) and to certain portions of the Madras Presidency. Under these arrangements, areas making up altogether about one-fifth of British India are permanently settled. In the remaining areas assessments are fixed for a period of years, the ordinary term at the present time being 30 years in Bombay, Madras, and the United Provinces, and 20 years in the Punjab and Central Provinces. In backward tracts, such as Burma and Assam, and in exceptional circumstances, such as exist in Sind, shorter terms have hitherto been permitted, but the 20-year period is being adopted in Burma and Assam.

The general features of the Land Revenue administration, whether *zamindari* or *ryotwari*, may be noted under three heads : (1) the preparation of the cadastral record, (2) the assessment of the revenue, and (3) the collection of the revenue so assessed. The processes coming under the first two heads are known collectively in most provinces as the "settlement" of the land revenue, and the officer who carries them out is known as the "Settlement Officer." During the last twenty or thirty years the object of shortening and simplifying settlement procedure has been kept steadily in view. Thus each province has a Land Records staff which, as is noted below, keeps the village maps and records up to date and preserves the survey boundary marks, and in other respects changes have been made that help to reduce the volume of work to be undertaken when a settlement is revised. Settlements, or re-settlements in new or in temporarily-settled areas are always in progress. In consequence of the attention now given to the maintenance of the village records, and of improved methods, the process occupies a much shorter period than formerly, and involves comparatively little harassment of the people. The duties of the assessing staff entail a minute local inspection from village to village through large tracts of country, and there are few officers of Government who are thrown more into contact with the people, or have greater opportunities of understanding their wants and feelings, than the settlement officers. Settlement operations of any importance are now everywhere carried out by members of the Indian Civil Service, or persons of like status, who are placed on special duty for the purpose.

The Cadastral Record and Record of Rights.—An essential preliminary to the assessment of land is the preparation of a cadastral map. In Bengal, where the revenue was permanently assessed in 1793, the assessment rests on information obtained without the aid of a survey; but this defect has given rise to inconvenience both fiscal and administrative, and it was found necessary in 1891 to introduce a cadastral survey and record in the Bihar districts in order to regulate the relations of landlord and tenant. In other provinces the existing assessments are based almost without exception on a field-to-field survey. The maps were, until recently, prepared in some instances by the scientific staff of the Survey Department, in others the skeleton data alone were so provided, the rest of the work being plotted by a local staff. All cadastral survey work is now done by the

Provincial Land Records and Settlement Department. A separate map is usually prepared for each "village." The cadastral map having been completed, the record of holdings is drawn up. This is primarily a fiscal record, the object of which is to show from whom the assessment of each holding is to be realised and the amount in each case. But the determination of these matters is closely bound up with the general question of land tenures, and it has been usual to supplement entries in this record, either by additional entries or by a separate record, in such a way as to show, to a greater or less extent, the existing rights in, and encumbrances on, the land. In most of the provinces where such a record-of-rights is prepared, it is given by law a presumptive force, being held to be correct until the contrary is proved. Arrangements are now in force in most provinces by which the cadastral records are revised either annually or at short intervals in such a way as to maintain the accuracy of the record, and there is thus being gradually built up a very extensive and complete system of registration of title by public entry.

The Assessment of the Land Revenue—The revenue is levied by means of a cash demand on each unit assessed. Under the *zamindari* system, the demand is assessed on the village or estate, which may be owned by a single proprietor, or by a proprietary body of co-sharers jointly responsible for payment of the revenue. The demand is a definite sum payable either in perpetuity or for a fixed term of years, during which the whole of any increased profits due to extension of cultivation, enhancement of rents, &c., is enjoyed by the individual landlord or the proprietary body. Under the *ryotwari* system, the assessment is on each field as demarcated by the cadastral survey. It takes the form of revenue rates for different classes of land, which are settled for a term of years, and, as the occupant may surrender any portion of his holding, or obtain an unoccupied field, the total sum payable by him as revenue may vary from year to year. The earliest cash assessments were the equivalents of fractional shares of the gross produce of the land, but it is unnecessary here to refer to the estimates that have been made of the fractions of the gross produce represented by the existing rates of land revenue, beyond saying that it is clear that Government now takes a very much lower share of the gross produce than was customary in pre-British days. Except in Bombay, where the assessment is not fixed in terms of the produce at all, the revenue throughout India is assessed so as to represent a share, not of the gross, but of the "net produce" (in *ryotwari* areas; "net assets" in *zamindari* areas). The meaning of the term "net produce" or "net assets" as employed for the purposes of assessment, varies in different parts of India. In Northern India and in the Central Provinces it represents the rent, where rent is paid, or that portion of the gross produce which would, if the land were rented, be taken by the landlord. In Madras and Lower Burma, on the other hand, where Government deals, as a rule, direct with the cultivator, the net produce is the difference between the assumed value of the gross produce and a very liberal estimate of the expense incurred in raising and disposing of the crop. Speaking generally, the "net assets" represent a larger share of the produce in Burma and Madras, where no middleman intervenes between the peasant-proprietor and the Government, than they do in Northern India. There is no hard and fast rule as to the proportion of the net assets to be taken as land revenue, but approximate standards, which differ somewhat from province to province, are laid down in the instructions to assessing officers. For India as a whole it may be said that the standard share of the calculated net assets or produce to be taken by Government is approximately one-half. Apart, however, from the fact that the net produce is usually calculated on very moderate lines, the share actually taken is more frequently below than above one-half. In the application of the standard rates to individual cases, considerable play is given to the working of local considerations and to the judgment and discretion of the assessing officer.

The distinguishing and essential feature of the assessments of Bombay is that they rest on the principle of adhering to what are known as "general considerations" rather than to statistical calculations of the soil, the economic conditions of the tract, the past revenue history, prices, and the selling, letting, and mortgage value of the land.

The general rule that the assessment is (for the term of a settlement) a fixed cash demand, representing the revenue fairly payable on an average of a series of seasons, is subject to some modification in precarious tracts, in regard to which the principle of a fluctuating assessment, by which the demand fluctuates year by year under rule, has been accepted and applied to some extent by most local Governments. The fluctuating assessment usually takes the form of acreage rates on the areas sown or matured in each harvest, the rates so imposed being, like the fixed lump assessment, unchangeable for a period of years.

In Madras there are "season remission rules", the effect of which is to adjust the revenue demand to some extent, particularly in the case of irrigated fields, to the character of the crop grown in a particular season.

Various provisions are made in the different provinces for exempting from assessment, either permanently or for a term of years, increases of income due to improvements such as, wells, tanks, and embankments made by private individuals, for the grant of favourable terms to cultivators who take up and clear waste land, for the avoidance of sudden enhancements of the land revenue demand, and for the relief from over-assessment of holdings which have suffered deterioration since they were assessed.

The Collection of the Revenue.—Little of a general nature need be said as to the collection of the revenue. Owing partly to the prevailing lack of capital among the agricultural population, the land revenue is generally recovered not by a single annual payment, but in instalments, the dates and amounts of which are fixed to meet local circumstances. For the recovery of sums not paid by due date the Government has extensive powers conferred by law. As a rule, a writ of demand or threat of attachment serves to bring about without further trouble the payment of such sums as are in arrear, and the more serious procedure of sale is comparatively seldom resorted to. Contumacious defaulters may be arrested and detained, but the number of persons actually confined is small.

Suspensions and Remissions.—It has been mentioned above that the rigidity of fixed assessments has been modified, and demand of each year apportioned more closely to the out-turn from which the demand is paid, to some extent, by the adoption of fluctuating assessments. In areas that are under a fixed assessment, although that assessment represents an amount fairly payable on an average, experience has shown that the land-holder cannot be counted on to lay by in good seasons enough to meet the revenue demand in very bad years, and it has been customary of late years in most provinces to grant with greater freedom, as necessity arises, a postponement of the whole or part of the demand on a harvest, and even, in cases where ultimate recovery would entail real hardship, to allow an absolute remission of the demand. Thus in 1899-1900 and 1900-01 the collection of revenue to the amount of £1,376,000 (over 2 crores) was suspended in the districts affected by famine, and at the conclusion of the famine in 1902, no less than £1,321,000 (198 lakhs) was entirely remitted. Over £500,000 (75 lakhs) was remitted in the United Provinces in 1908.

The Government of India in a Resolution dated the 25th March 1905 laid down the principles to be followed by local Governments in order to bring the local rules for the suspension and remission of land revenue into conformity. The general view expressed was that while it was wholesome and legitimate to expect the cultivator to take the bad with the good in years of ordinary fluctuation, it was hopeless to expect him to be able to meet the fixed demand in years when the crops barely suffice for his own sustenance, and that payments should not be enforced under conditions which would compel a cultivator of ordinary care and prudence to imperil his future solvency in order to meet them. General rules for carrying this view into effect in various circumstances were laid down. It was decided to adhere to the conclusion arrived at in 1882 (when previous instructions for modifying, where necessary, the strict system of revenue assessment and collection were issued) and endorsed by the Famine Commission of 1901, that "relief will not ordinarily be required when there is half a normal crop." On the other hand it was suggested that total relief should be given where the crop is less than a quarter of the normal. The principle was accepted that, as a general rule, no suspended revenue should be collected until after one fair harvest subsequent to the failure has been reaped in the affected tract. It was further laid down that, no relief should ordinarily be given to the revenue-payer of the landlord class unless it can be ensured either by legislation or by arrangement that a proportionate degree of relief will be extended to the actual cultivators of the soil, or at least to the tenant class. Local Governments were requested to examine their existing rules in the light of the various principles now laid down, by the adoption of which, the Government of India believed, the administration of the fixed land revenue system of India would be freed from the evils of excessive rigidity that had in some places hitherto attached to it, and a degree of elasticity would be introduced sufficient to ensure that in times of agricultural calamity the burdens of the cultivating classes would not be aggravated by any unreasonable insistence on the demands of Government.

II.—Revenue Surveys and Settlements and Land Records.

Extracts from the Report on the Moral and Material Progress of India, Decennial Issue, 1913, pp. 175-79.

Bengal, Bihar and Orissa and Assam.—The greater part of the land revenue of Bengal (including Bihar and Orissa) was permanently settled at the end of the eighteenth century. At the present time the land revenue in Bengal represents less than a quarter of the total rental. The settlement of 1793 did not extend to the whole province, and the tracts then omitted, as well as those acquired since, such as Orissa and Darjeeling, and also many alluvial islands and estates that have escheated, or have been purchased from time to time by Government at revenue sales, are temporarily settled. The power to order a survey and record-of-rights in any local area was given by the Bengal Tenancy Act of 1885; the institution of operations in the permanently settled tracts was a most important step, the object being to frame an authoritative record of the status and rents of the tenants, with a view to protect them against arbitrary eviction and illegal enhancement, and to compose or avert agrarian disputes. It is reported that the manifold advantages secured by the preparation of a trustworthy map and record-of-rights are now generally acknowledged, both by landlords and tenants. In September 1902 the total area for which a record-of-rights had been completed was 29,610 square miles, out of a total of 151,185 square miles of British territory in Bengal, as then defined. By September 1911 the record-of-rights had been completed for 64,805 square miles out of the reduced total area of 116,175 square miles. The areas dealt with by the Settlement Department in Bengal during the decade thus fell mainly under four heads: (1) temporarily settled estates, where a settlement of land revenue and rents is necessary in addition to the record-of-rights; (2) permanently settled estates in the Sonthal Parganas, where, besides the preparation of a record-of-rights, the rent of every tenant had to be settled, (3) other permanently settled tracts, where the work consists of the preparation of a record-of-rights and the decision of agrarian disputes, the settlement of fair rents being made only on the application of landlords or tenants; and (4) the temporarily settled portion of Orissa, in which the revision of the last cadastral survey and record-of-rights was taken in hand in 1906 in order to bring them up to date with a view to their being then continuously maintained. The survey and preparation of a record-of-rights in the Sonthal Parganas, begun in 1898, were completed in 1910. The rent of every tenant and headman in this large area (over 5,000 square miles) was thus settled, and the respective rights of landlord, headman, and ryot in every village clearly defined. The result was an increase of about Rs. 90,000 a year in the Government revenue, while private proprietors also obtained material enhancements of their rent-rolls. Rent-rates are nevertheless still low, and the rents are reported to be paid cheerfully in all cases.

In Eastern Bengal, as in Bengal, it is now the settled policy of Government to prepare and keep up to date a record-of-rights not only where the land revenue is subject to periodical revision, but also throughout the whole permanently settled area. Up to September 1911, the cadastral survey and record-of-rights had been completed in 8,109 square miles in Eastern Bengal, and 9,369 square miles in Assam, and operations were in progress during 1910-11 in a further area of 8,385 square miles in Eastern Bengal; the outstanding areas were 23,345 square miles in Eastern Bengal and 27,152 square miles in Assam.

In Assam only a comparatively small part of the country is permanently settled, the rest being Government property; the ordinary land tenures vary considerably in different parts, while several varieties of special waste land tenures, granted by Government at different periods, exist in all the plains districts. In the Sylhet and Goalpara districts a large proportion of the area is permanently settled. The distinguishing features of the agricultural system of Assam proper are the large areas of unsettled waste land, and the system under which in certain tracts land is cultivated for two or three years and then resigned. These two conditions necessitate a simple system of land revenue administration, the ryots holding under an annual or decennial lease from Government. In the hill districts there is, except in a few isolated tracts, no land revenue settlement properly so called. The ordinary form of taxation in these parts is a house-tax. The decennial settlement of the Assam Valley districts being about to expire, re-settlement operations were inaugurated in 1902 on a new system, known as the "soil-unit" system, by which the assessment of the land revenue is, as far as possible, fixed by the people themselves, with reference to the popular estimate of the relative values of the different classes of soils and of the relative natural advantages of different areas. In none of the districts was the revenue demand greatly enhanced in the Kamrup district, which was leniently treated in view of the severity of the effects of the earthquake of 1897; the final result was a total abatement of $2\frac{1}{3}$ per cent.

United Provinces.—In the Benares Division the land revenue was permanently settled, at the end of the eighteenth century. Elsewhere in the United Provinces the ordinary term of a settlement is thirty years. In the assessment of revenue the rule is that the State demand should be, approximately, one-half of the rental "assets."

The second regular settlement in Oudh was carried out between 1893 and 1903. Extensive re-settlement operations were carried through also in Agra in the earlier years of the decade, (1902-1911), the results varying between an increase of the revenue-demand to the extent of 34 per cent. in Meerut and a decrease of over 14 per cent. in Cawnpore. In Bundelkhund the settlement was revised under special rules, providing for a fluctuating assessment. Regular settlements were in progress in two districts during the year ending in September 1912. The department of land records was credited with steady and improved work, and it was decided, in connection with settlements recently commenced, to dispense with a professional survey and to accept the existing maps corrected and brought up to date by the *patwaris.*

Punjab.—In the Punjab, as in Bengal and the United Provinces, the system of land tenures is that known as *zamindari.* The *zamindars* in an entire estate are technically bound by a common responsibility towards Government in the matter of the land revenue, but the tendency is towards individualism, and with lighter and more elastic assessments the enforcement of collective responsibility has become practically obsolete. In practice the owner, or owners, of each holding is, or are, assessed separately. The term of a settlement is now usually 30 years in the case of fully developed districts, and 20 years where conditions are less advanced. There has been a considerable extension, in recent years, especially on river-side areas and in rainless tracts of the Western Punjab, of the "fluctuating" system of assessment, under which the fixed cash assessment is replaced by cash acreage rates on the actual area cropped at each harvest. The assessment is calculated on the net "assets," but competition rents are rarely paid in cash, and in the more usual case of kind-rents the value of the "assets" can be arrived at only after a number of elaborate and somewhat uncertain calculations as to prices, yields, etc. Although, therefore, the standard of assessment is represented, as in the United Provinces, by one-half the net "assets," the standard is looked upon not as determining the average assessment, but as fixing an outside maximum. The assessments in the Punjab have generally been noted for their moderation. A return laid before Parliament in 1908* gave in detail the results of settlement operations in the Punjab from 1855 onwards. It showed that the rate of land revenue per cultivated acre, measured in rupees, had not varied much, and that its incidence measured in gold had therefore greatly decreased.

Madras.—Nearly a third of the Madras Presidency, made up of districts in the north, is permanently settled on the *zamindari* system. Over the rest of the Presidency (leaving out of account the comparatively small areas held under various special tenures) *ryotwari* tenure prevails. The basis of the latter system is the division of the whole area into fields, each field being valued at a fixed rate per acre and the assessment settled thereon. The first stage is soil classification, certain food-staples are then selected as representative, and the average out-turn is ascertained by numerous measurements, the out-turns are valued by a commutation-rate rather—sometimes much—below the average of prices for the previous 20 non-famine years; large deductions are made for the difference between market and village prices, and for vicissitudes of season and unprofitable patches, and the expenses of cultivation are subtracted. The "net produce" being thus arrived at, a nominal half (usually less) gives the rate of the assessment applicable to the particular soil in question. Finally the rates are compared with the existing rates and reduced if necessary. The amounts paid for sub-leases indicate that the nominal half is actually often a fourth, and, on the richer lands, a sixth or even less

* Cd. 3991 of 1908.

proportion of the net produce. The term of settlement is 30 years. An annual settlement of accounts is held to ascertain and record any changes in the holdings, and any remissions under the "season remission rules" that exist in Madras.

Bombay.—In Bombay Presidency, outside Sind, the land revenue system is with few exceptions *ryotwari*, the settlement being with cultivators of small holdings whose revenue payments are fixed after careful measurement and classification of their lands. The assessment is based on a classification of fields according to soil, situation, and natural defects, such as liability to inundation and the like. The fields being classed, villages are grouped with reference to their nearness to markets, to means of communication, and other economic conditions. Maximum rates for the groups are fixed with regard to these considerations and to average prices. The assessment on any field is then determined as a proportion of the maximum depending upon the class to which it belongs. The term of a settlement is 30 years. Since 1884 it has been laid down as a general rule that at revision settlements the increase of revenue shall not exceed 100 per cent. on an individual holding, 66 per cent. on a village, or 33 per cent. on a group of villages. Besides the *ryotwari* tenure, there are a number of other forms of tenure. In Sind the land is held by a large number of peasant occupants, and by a small body, numerically, of large proprietors. Practically the whole of Sind is now under what is known as the irrigational settlement, which included the charge for irrigation water under land revenne. The assessment is based on the mode of irrigation adopted. The special feature of the Sind settlement is the allowance for fallows, which are common owing to the poorness of the soil, the abundance of waste land, and the absence of a sufficient supply of manure. Occupants are liable to the full assessment on each survey number when cultivated, but fallow lands are free provided that assessment is paid thereon once in five years. The term of a settlement in Sind is 10 years.

The record-of-rights, which was introduced into the Presidency under an Act (the Bombay Land Record-of-Rights Act) passed in 1903 is being maintained and kept up to date by mutation registers. In most districts the record has produced a marked diminution in litigation, and in petty crime arising out of land disputes.

III.—Tenant Right and Land Legislation.

Extracts from the Report on the Moral and Material Progress of India, Decennial Issue, 1913, pp. 175, 183—188.

Tenant-Right.—By the ancient custom of India the occupiers of the soil had the right to retain their holdings, so long as they paid the rent or revenue demandable from them. In Southern India, where most of the land is held by petty occupiers direct from the State, this custom has been respected from the beginning of British rule; and in both the permanently and temporarily settled districts of Northern India a considerable degree of protection has now been given to the tenants or ryots. Up to 1859 tenant-right had not been adequately safe-guarded by law, and for the great province of Bengal, the Court of Directors reported in 1858 that "the rights of the Bengal ryots had passed away *sub silentio*, and they had become, to all intents and purposes, tenants-at-will." Since 1858 laws have been passed which make the petty occupiers of Madras, Bombay, Burma, and Assam proprietors of their holdings, subject to the payment of a moderate land revenue; and the petty proprietors are protected against future enhancements of land revenue on account of improvements effected by themselves. For nearly every other province in India laws have been passed securing tenant-right to all occupiers of any standing, prohibiting eviction or enhancement of rent, save by consent or by decree of court, on good cause shown, and granting the ryots power to bequeath or sell their tenant-right.

The extent and character of the tenant-right declared or created by these laws vary in the different provinces; tenant-right is strongest in the Central Provinces, where the old land tenures were not very unlike the petty proprietorships of Bombay; it is less important in the

Punjab, where the bulk of the land is occupied by proprietary brotherhoods, and the holdings of rent-paying tenants are comparatively small; and it is weak in Oudh, where the position of the taluqdars or superior proprietors was exceptionally strong, and had been confirmed by the British Government. The position of tenants or occupiers in every province is better and more secure than it was fifty years ago. In permanently settled Bengal, the Tenancy Act of 1885 has greatly strengthened and improved the position of the ryot ; and the cadastral survey which is being carried out in the province shows that the great bulk of the ryots enjoy tenant-right under the law. Thus LORD CORNWALLIS' intention in favour of the ryots, promulgated more than 100 years ago, has, so far as changed circumstances permitted, been at last carried into effect, for the rights of the occupiers of the soil have been in great part secured ; and this has been done without injustice to the Bengal landlords, whose gross rental has increased four or five fold during the century, and has in many tracts more than doubled during the past fifty years.

Throughout considerable parts of India, it may be added, the Government has power to ensure the suspension or remission of rent to meet cases of crop-failure.

Bengal, Bihar and Orissa, and Assam.—Throughout the greater part of Bengal (including Bihar and Orissa) the relations of landlord and tenant are governed by the Bengal Tenancy Act of 1885, which secured the status and privileges of all classes of tenants. The Act provides that every ryot who has held any land in a village for 12 years acquires thereby a right of occupancy, and 80 or 90 per cent. of ryots have such rights. A small number of ryots hold at fixed rates of rent, and the remainder are without right of occupancy. Even the latter, however, cannot be ejected except in execution of the decree of a competent court, nor can their rents be enhanced at shorter intervals than five years. The Act was amended by Bengal Act I of 1907, with the object of giving greater facilities to landlords for the collection of rent, and at the same time of guarding against enhancement of rent by collusive compromises, and removing the ambiguities, anomalies, and defects brought to light by twenty years' experience of the working of the Act. Its main provisions are now fairly well known both to landlords and to tenants; but there are indications that the importance of various sections has not yet been realised by the public. The levy of *abwabs* or illegal cesses in addition to rent continues to prevail more of less throughout the Presidency. It is reported that, as a rule, the tenants pay these illegal demands without much demur in order to escape harassment in other ways.

For the Chota Nagpur Division, the law as to landlord and tenant was consolidated and amended by the Chota Nagpur Tenancy Act of 1908, the object of which was to secure the ryots in the enjoyment of their existing rights, and to ensure in cases of necessity their protection against oppressive landlords, while at the same time safe-guarding the interests of the landlords in many important matters. It was reported in 1911 that as a result of the application of this Act to the evidence afforded by the record-of-rights, the burdens of litigation and of general administration had decreased enormously, and that there was now abroad a feeling of security in the enjoyment of agrarian rights. The Act is as yet imperfectly understood by the aborigines of the division, and is being cautiously administered, with good results.

The Government of Bengal came to the conclusion, towards the end of the decade, (1902-1911) that it was desirable to undertake special legislation also for three of the districts of the Orissa Division. There was evidence to show that the sections of the Bengal Tenancy Act applied to those districts had proved in practice to be ill-adapted to local conditions. The revisional settlement had brought to light the fact that claims by landlords to a record in their own names of lands alleged to be in their cultivating possession, were frequent, and that disputes on this subject between them and their tenants were acute. It was found also that agreements were often exacted from tenants the effect of which was to prevent the accrual of occupancy rights, and that a large majority of landlords were opposing the reclamation of waste lands by cultivators, and, where such reclamations had been made, were endeavouring to deprive the cultivators of the fruits of their labour. The Orissa Tenancy Bill, introduced in the Bengal Legislative Council in July 1911, was intended to remedy these and other defects, and to provide a new self-contained agrarian code for the districts in question; it made provision also for the maintenance of land records. The Bill was finally passed by the Bengal Legislative Council on the 27th March 1912, four days before the new province of Bihar and Orissa was constituted. In view of this last fact, and of the contentious nature of the Bill, the Governor-General withheld his assent, so as to leave the Government and the Legislative Council of the new province free to deal with the various questions raised.

The Bengal Tenancy Act is in force in all the Eastern Bengal districts, except the Chittagong Hill Tracts. It was amended in 1908, as regards Eastern Bengal, by an Act following the same lines as the Bengal Act of 1907.

In Assam the only special law as to landlord and tenant is the Landlord and Tenant Procedure Act of 1869, which is in force in Goalpara and Sylhet.

United Provinces.—Questions of tenancy-right and rent-rates are of great importance in the United Provinces, as in Bengal. The bulk of the land is held by cash-paying tenants, and except in the permanently-settled area the revenue is assessed on the basis of the rents in force at the time of settlement. In the permanently-settled districts a special class of tenants is found who have heritable and transferable rights at a fixed rent, and are liable to eviction only for default in paying rent. Other tenants are divided into two classes according as they have or have not a right of occupancy ; but the term "occupancy tenant" bears different meanings in Agra and Oudh.

In Agra the occupancy tenant has a heritable right to hold certain land, and is not liable to eviction except for default in paying rent, while the rent payable cannot be enhanced except by mutual agreement or by order of revenue court, generally on the ground that it is below the prevailing standard of rent for similar land. Since 1859 any tenant has acquired occupancy rights in land cultivated from year to year without a lease for at least 12 years, and an Act of 1901 (the Agra Tenancy Act), provides that the change of a holding or dispossession for less than a year shall not operate as a break in the period of 12 years, while a lease does not prevent the accrual of occupancy rights unless it is for at least seven years, the object being to induce landlords, if they do not choose that their tenants shall acquire any rights, at least to grant them long-term leases. The Act also made the ejectment of ordinary tenants more difficult. The number of ejectments has nevertheless risen in recent years ; but, on the other hand, the area protected from arbitrary ejectment by long leases or occupancy rights has grown considerably, and amounted in 1911 to 68 per cent. of the total area held by ordinary tenants as compared with 64 per cent. in 1903.

A land-holder who parts with his proprietary rights obtains occupancy rights in his home farm at a privileged rate of rent, 25 per cent. below the rate generally payable by non-occupancy tenants. This is called "ex-proprietary right."

In Oudh the so-called "occupancy tenant" corresponds to the "ex-proprietary tenant" in Agra, and no tenant acquires occupancy rights by prescription; the rent of the occupancy tenant cannot be enhanced beyond a rate $12\frac{1}{2}$ per cent. lower than that ordinarily paid by cultivators with no such right.

Other tenants in Agra are merely tenants-at-will, but the Act provides that, where the rent of a non-occupancy tenant is enhanced, he shall be entitled, as a general rule, to hold the land at the enhanced rent for a term of not less than five years. In Oudh any person admitted to the cultivation of land acquires certain rights; he is entitled to hold it for seven years at the same rent, and enhancement at the end of that period is limited to $6\frac{1}{4}$ per cent.

Laws passed in recent years have placed important restrictions on the transfer of land. The Oudh Settled Estates Act of 1900 provided a system of entail, which can, however, be applied only in the case of *taluqdars* and grantees whose estates are subject to the rule of primogeniture. In 1903 special legislation was undertaken for Bundelkhund, in view of the serious indebtedness of the land-holders of this tract, in which great liability to agricultural calamity is coupled with markedly improvident habits on the part of the people. The first Act (the Bundelkhund Incumbered Estates Act, 1903) revived and extended, with modifications, legislation applied to Jhansi in 1882, which provided for inquiry into debts by a special judge, and for liquidation of the amounts found to be justly due with the aid of loans from Government. At the same time, and as a necessary complement, restrictions were placed upon the right of transfer by a second measure (the Bundelkhund Alienation of Land Act, 1903) modelled on the Punjab Act of 1901. Under this Act permanent alienations of land cannot be made, without the special sanction of the Collector, where the alienor is a member of one of certain agricultural tribes, except in favour of another member of the same tribe or when both parties reside in the same district and are both members of agricultural tribes. Except when permanent alienation is allowed mortgages and leases are subject to the condition that possession of the land involved cannot be transferred for more than 20 years. Sales in execution of decrees passed by civil or revenue courts (other than those of the Special Judges appointed) are forbidden, but such decrees may be liquidated by usufructuary mortgages for terms not exceeding 20 years. The Act is reported to be working satisfactorily. The price of land is gradually rising, and there is no general dissatisfaction with the Act on the ground of depreciation of land value. It is reported from some parts that the agricultural classes are learning to exercise economy in marriage and other expenses, because they cannot get loans as easily as before, and that their financial condition has much improved in consequence.

Punjab.—As nearly one-half of the land in the Punjab is cultivated by the owners themselves, and a fair proportion of the rest by owners who pay rent to co-sharers or other owners, the tenant class is neither so large nor so distinctively marked as in the rest of Northern India, and the law affords much less elaborate protection to the tenant than is usual in the United Provinces or in Bengal. A limited number of the class, amounting to nearly one-fifth of the whole, have been marked off by the legislature on certain historical grounds as entitled to rights of occupancy, and the rents of his class cannot be enhanced beyond a standard fixed in each case with reference to the land revenue. In the case of the remaining tenants, who hold at will, no limit is fixed to the discretion of the landlord in the matter of enhancement, but the procedure to be followed in ejectment, and the grant of compensation for improvements legally executed, are provided for by law in respect of both classes of tenants. The question of the alienation of land, on the other hand, has in the Punjab taken a prominent place. In view of the serious extent to which land was passing from the hands of the old agricultural tribes to those of the moneyed classes, the Government was compelled in 1901 to place restrictions on the alienation of land in the province. The Act passed (the Punjab Alienation of Land Act, 1901*) was the first general measure of its kind introduced in India, and one of the greatest importance. Experience of the working of the Act has shown that it has been a great success, and that, though there has been some contraction of credit and a welcome reduction in extravagant expenditure, the *zamindar* has not been hampered in his business or in his daily life by any difficulty in getting ready money

* The provisions of the Punjab Alienation of Land Act are briefly as follows :—Permanent alienation of agricultural land is permitted without restriction when the alienor is not a member of an agricultural tribe, or when a member of an agricultural tribe alienates to an agriculturist holding land in the same village, or to another member of his own tribe or group of tribes. In any other case, excepting religious and charitable gifts, inquiry is to be made by a revenue officer, who must not be lower in rank than a Deputy Commissioner, and sanction given or withheld at his discretion. It is to be observed that there is nothing absolute about this restriction. As was said by the Lieutenant-Governor when the Bill was under discussion, "The person who lies under the greatest disability under the proposed Bill can obtain a dispensation from its provisions, if due cause be shown." Temporary alienations by agriculturists to persons outside their agricultural tribes are only permitted under the Act in the form of usufructuary mortgages for a maximum period of 20 years, on the expiry of which the land reverts to the mortgagor and the debt is cancelled. The Act applies to the Punjab generally, saving such tracts as may be specially exempted under the powers given by it. This is one of the most important legislative measures which the Indian Government has ever passed not only as affecting profoundly the conditions of cultivating ownership throughout the Punjab, but also as being likely to serve as a model for other provinces where the expropriation of the peasantry by the money-lender is a social and political danger. (*Moral and Material Progress and Condition of India, 1892-93 to 1901-02.*)

when he requires it. Some amendments in matters of detail were made by an Act passed in 1907. It is reported that the most interesting phenomenon at present is the endeavour of those who are not members of agricultural tribes notified under the Act, and see no prospect of notification, to alter their tribal designation to that of a scheduled tribe. Attempts to evade the Act, with the aid of dummy transferees, or by other means, come to notice and require careful watching. Between 1901-02 and 1911-12 there was a steady rise in the average sale price of land from less than Rs. 75 to over Rs. 120 per cultivated acre.

One of the corollaries to the passing of the Alienation of Land Act was the recasting of the law of pre-emption. The new law came into force as the Punjab Pre-emption Act of 1905, its chief aim being to prevent a non-agriculturist when he has once gained a footing in a village community from buying up other shares in the village as they come into the market and so expropriating the true agriculturist and breaking up the village community. The pre-emption law is admittedly unsatisfactory, and gives rise to abuses, and there is a considerable body of opinion in favour of sweeping away the whole system as an archaic survival.

Madras.—In the *ryotwari* areas in Madras the registered occupant of each field is entitled to hold the land for ever (subject to the possibility of purchase for a public purpose) so long as he pays his land revenue, and inheritance, transfer, mortgage, sale, and lease are without restriction. Registered ryots in many cases sub-let their lands. The distribution of the land among the several classes, the character of the people, and the comparative absence of professional money-lenders of an alien class, have rendered unnecessary any legislation or measures directed against the acquisition of land by non-agricultural classes.

The status and rights of the cultivators in *zamindari* estates were not in the past everywhere clear, though in most cases they were fixed upon the land precisely like *ryotwari* cultivators. The *zamindars*, however, usually have home-farm land, in which they possess complete rights, and can demand any rents they can obtain. The position of tenants in the *zamindari* areas is now defined and regulated by the Madras Estates Land Act of 1908. This important measure repealed and re-enacted the processual enactment, the Madras Rent Recovery Act, 1865, and at the same time remedied the imperfections of the old Act and declared in clear terms the substantive and relative rights of land-holders and ryots. In respect of the most important of the ryot's rights, that of occupancy, the Act proceeds upon the principle that every cultivator admitted by the land-holder to the cultivation of the estate lands (not being private domain or land of the description classed as "old waste") has the status of an occupancy ryot protected against eviction so long as he pays the established or prescribed rates of rent. This was the position enjoyed by the cultivator under ancient custom. The occupancy tenure is heritable and transferable. Enhancement of rent is permitted only within certain limits and on certain clearly defined grounds, and then only by suit before the Collector. A non-occupancy ryot may acquire occupancy rights by the payment of a sum equal to $2\frac{1}{2}$ years' rent. Non-occupancy ryots also are protected in respect of enhancement of rents and ejectment. The Act further makes provision for the maintenance by the land-holder of irrigation works, the survey of estates, the preparation of a record-of-rights, and the settlement of rents, and for the ousting of the original jurisdiction of civil courts in disputes between land-holders and ryots. The immediate effect of the Act in some districts was disturbing, and it led to considerable litigation, but it is reported that difficulties are gradually settling down as suits are decided and as the provisions of the Act are better understood.

Mention may also be made of the Madras Land Encroachment Act of 1905, which provided for the prevention of the unauthorised occupation of public lands, and for the levy of charges in respect of such occupation.

Bombay.—In Bombay, as in Madras, a ryot is secured in possession of his holding so long as he regularly pays the instalments of his land revenue, and the right of occupancy, in the case of the ordinary survey tenure, is transferable by inheritance, sale, gift, or mortgage without restriction. In Sind few tenant-rights are in existence. The smaller *zamindars* cultivate for themselves, and the larger through yearly tenants, who almost always pay rent in kind. Two important enactments have a special bearing on the land revenue policy of the Bombay Government. In 1879 the Deccan Agriculturists' Relief Act was passed to cope with agrarian discontent in four Deccan Districts,—Poona, Satara, Sholapur, and Ahmednagar. The Act provided for the appointment of a special judge and numerous conciliators, who were empowered to investigate mortgages and similar alienations of land, to revise the terms of the contract, and to arrange for an equitable settlement of claims, with a view to restoring the original rights of the occupant. The greater part of the Act was extended to the remainder of the Presidency, except Aden and the City of Bombay, in 1905. Reports indicate that the Act has had the desired effect of protecting the revenue-paying classes from the encroachment of non-agriculturists, and that, although it has restricted credit, it has not done so to the extent of hampering agricultural operations. The Bombay Land Revenue Code Amendment Act of 1901 created a special tenure known as the restricted or non-transferable tenure. Under this Act the Collector is authorised to grant the occupancy of lands for limited periods or on such conditions as he may think necessary, the principle of these being that the occupant cannot alienate his land without the previous permission of the Collector. The total area held under the restricted tenure on the 31st July 1911 was 2,191 square miles. The conditions of non-alienable tenure are designed to meet the circumstances of the wild tribes, the depressed castes, and other classes of cultivators who are known to be backward or improvident.

IV —SETTLEMENT AND CADASTRAL SURVEYS.

Based on the Moral and Material Progress Report, 1899-1900, and Decennial Report, 1883-1892.

The term "settlement" is applied in Indian revenue affairs to the process of assessing the land revenue demand. Occasionally, in newly acquired or specially backward tracts, the land revenue is assessed for a short term of years on a general review of the circumstances and capabilities of the land and people concerned; such a process is called a summary settlement. But a regular settlement is a more complicated affair, and consists of many stages. In the first place, every separate estate or holding is demarcated by permanent marks on the ground, and disputes between neighbouring right-holders are investigated and decided. Every estate or holding is then surveyed and mapped, all boundary marks, wells, and buildings being shown on the field or cadastral maps. A record is at the same time drawn up of all rents paid, and of all rights, whether landlord rights, or tenant rights, or rights of user, over all the ground, buildings, wells, and trees shown in the map.

In provinces where the *zamindari* tenure prevails, that is, where single proprietors or proprietary brotherhoods possess large estates of several hundreds or thousands of acres, the State revenue is assessed at an aliquot part (usually about one-half) of the ascertained or the assumed rental. The revenue, though it is fixed with reference to acreage rates on the land actually cultivated, is assessed on, and is payable by, each estate as a whole; the assessment remains unchanged for the thirty years or other period of the settlement; the proprietor can bring as much as he likes of his waste or fallow land under the plough; and it is only on re-assessment at the end of the term of the settlement that the State obtains any increase of revenue on account of the extensions of cultivation during the settlement period. In provinces where the *ryotwari* tenure prevails, that is, where each petty proprietor holds directly from the State, generally cultivates his own land, and has no landlord between himself and the Government, the revenue is separately assessed at an acreage rate on each petty holding, and land revenue becomes payable at once, or after a short term of grace in the case of uncleared lands, on all extensions of cultivation. The *ryotwari* proprietor is at liberty to throw up his holding or any portion of it, at the beginning of any year, after reasonable notice; the *zamindar* or large proprietor engages to pay the revenue assessed upon him for the term of the settlement.

After the revenue is assessed and the assessment is sanctioned, copies of the field map, of the schedule of fields, and of the record-of-rights are made, one copy is given to the proprietor, one copy is lodged in the district court house, and usually a third copy is placed in the sub-divisional or tahsil office. Through the agency of the local officials of each village or circle the field maps and record-of-rights are corrected or written up year by year, so as to make them at all times faithful accounts of current rural facts and circumstances. When revisions of assessment are undertaken at the end of the settlement, the village maps and records serve, after adequate testings and corrections, as the basis for re-assessment, and in this way a re-settlement is a shorter and less costly affair, and causes much less harassment to the people than is involved in an original settlement.

The internal boundary marks, too, are of more importance under the individual settlement system than when the village is the unit of settlement, so the maps of the village in the former case are more elaborate. In most of Bengal the survey operations are different in scope from those in Provinces where the assessment is periodically revised, and, except in tracts not under the Permanent Settlement, are chiefly concerned with estates under the temporary management of the State, or which have lapsed or which, again, are under periodical settlements. There is also a considerable amount of work found every year in the survey of the tracts affected by the great changes that are annually liable to occur in the courses of the numerous estuaries, leading to questions of alluvion, diluvion, and the formation of new islands, which affect miles of country, and to which is attributed much of the rioting and allied offences in Eastern Bengal.

The next step in the process is the classification of the villages under settlement into groups, or assessment circles, according to similarity in their general conditions, such as distinctions of soil, altitude, rainfall, fluvial action, and so on, sometimes with internal re-grouping with reference to communications, water supply, or proximity to markets. The process is carried a stage further in each village, since the soil has to be classified, either by homogeneous blocks, as in parts of Upper India, or field by field, as in Madras and Bombay. Speaking generally, natural qualities are distinguished from artificial such as those resulting from manure, or rather from the facilities for receiving that fertilising agent. Even where this is not done explicitly the distinction is often marked by the nomenclature adopted in recording the description of the soil under inspection. Irrigated lands are distinguished from the rest, and in Bombay a special provision was introduced during the decade 1883-92 relating to sub-soil water-bearing qualities, irrespective of the actual use of the advantage.

The whole of the information relative to the villages comprised in the assessment circle is compiled and analysed by the Settlement Officer. The past fiscal history of the tract is reviewed in relation to the extension of cultivation, variations in prices, and rents, in the stock of plough and milch cattle, improvement or communications and various other general considerations, on which the revenue or rent-rate, as the case may be, is based. In connection with this most important duty, rules were passed between 1883 and 1885 by the Government of India, after consultation with the local authorities in each Province, setting forth the general principles on which future enhancements of assessment should alone be made. To some extent the provisions only confirmed existing practice, but the main point was the substitution of general considerations, ascertainable from the current revenue records, for the expense, delay, and general inconvenience to both State and public of fresh valuation of produce, rental or soil, at the expiration of each term of settlement. The three grounds on which enhancement is now generally speaking permissible are (*a*) Increase of the area under cultivation, (*b*) Rise in prices of agricultural produce, and (*c*) Increase in produce, due directly or indirectly to improvements effected at the expense of the State, or from public resources. Improvements effected by the cultivators or landed classes themselves, whether from their own funds or by means of personal State loans, and whether arising from improved methods of tillage or otherwise, had always been held exempt from assessment in most, though not all, parts of India, but the rules in question extended the exemption throughout the country. The most importent question that arose in connection with the above rules was that of the initial assessment which was to be taken as the basis of future revision. Where the earlier operations proved accurate and experience showed the settlement to have been successful from the point of view of both parties concerned, the State and the cultivator or proprietor, it was obviously superfluous to conduct afresh similar investigation. But in some cases the former record was known to be inadequate as to both survey measurements and valuation, so that here the revision necessarily included that of the preliminary operations. When once the initial assessment is settled satisfactorily, the main duty that devolves upon the local officials under the current scheme is that of keeping the village record up to date, so that re-settlement, when it falls due, may be made from it, irrespective of fresh detailed investigation. This involves the annual correction of the village map under all systems, such as those of Upper India, in which the whole of the unoccupied land in a village is not surveyed, demarcated, and assessed at the time of settlement. In the Madras and Bombay settlements the map is written up once for all. Then there is the record of occupancy to be similarly kept up, according to the requirements of the Provincial system. In Upper India more detail is entered as regards the land in occupation than under the system of individual settlements, where the State looks no further than the registered occupant, and disregards, as a rule, subordinate rights. Assuming that the local duties are efficiently fulfilled, it has been estimated that a saving of over two-thirds the expenditure on re-settlement will ultimately be effected by the adoption of the above system. The method of arriving at the initial assessment, varies greatly in the different Provinces. The preliminary processes have furnished the Settlement Officer, as above remarked with full information as to the relative productive value, by soil groups, of each village in Upper India, and of each field in Southern and Western Presidencies, in addition to the more general statistics as to the material circumstances of the population of the tract to be dealt with.

BENGAL.

Based on the Administration Report of Bengal, 1911-12.

Permanent Settlement, 1793.—With the exception of some parts which are temporarily settled the land revenue in Bengal is fixed under the Permanent Settlement concluded by LORD CORNWALLIS in 1793. The East India Company succeeded to the *Dewani* of Bengal, Bihar and Orissa in 1765, and it was not till 1771 that they assumed, by the agency of their own servants, the direct management of the revenues. When, as a result of the grant of the *Dewani*, it became necessary for the Company's servants to undertake the administration of the land revenue, they were placed in one of the most extraordinary positions recorded in history. Having been solely occupied in the pursuit of trade, they had no previous means of acquiring that knowledge and experience which were necessary to enable them to take with confidence the helm of affairs. The whole theory of Indian land revenue was unknown to them, nor was there a system of written rules and plain principles which they could learn by careful application. "The Company's servants," as MR. KAYE says, "were dead hands at investments, but they knew nothing of land tenures." Accordingly, the revenue was for some years collected on the old Moghul system. The *zamindars*, or Government farmers, were recognized as having a right to collect the revenue from the actual cultivators, but no principle of assessment existed. The assessments were made for five years at one period, and for one year at another; while abuses prevailed as much in the collection of the revenue due to Government as in the realization of the rents due to *zamindars*. It was the object of LORD CORNWALLIS, almost from the moment of his arrival, to enquire into these abuses, to redress grievances, and to provide for the well-being of the cultivating community, the security of the *zamindars*, and the interest of the East India Company, by one equitable code and system. With this object in view, the Decennial Settlement was commenced in 1789 and completed in 1791. LORD CORNWALLIS advocated the making of this settlement permanent at once, but the Court of Directors, knowing that SHORE and other able advisers deprecated the immediate declaration of permanence, deliberated for two years, and it was not till September 1792 that they consented to the proposal. A proclamation was then issued on the 22nd March, 1793, by which the Governor-General in Council declared that the *zamindars*, independent *taluqdars* and other actual proprietors of land, with whom the Decennial Settlement had been concluded, would be allowed to hold their estates at the same assessment for ever, but that "no claims for remission or suspension of rent were to be admitted on any account, and lands of proprietors were to be invariably sold for arrears." Proprietors were also declared to have the privilege of transferring their lands without the sanction of Government, and partition or division of estates was to be freely allowed. This proclamation was afterwards included in the Statute Book as Regulation 1 of 1793.

Permanently settled tracts.—The Permanent Settlement embraced, roughly speaking, the tracts of country now included in the Burdwan, the Presidency, Patna, Bhagalpore, Rajshahi, Dacca and Chittagong Divisions. It also comprised parts of the Hazaribagh and Manbhum districts and a few estates in Singbhum and Ranchi in the Chota Nagpur Division, as well as Goalpara and Sylhet.

Resumption proceedings.—At the time of the Permanent Settlement large areas were claimed as revenue free and the authority to scrutinize such revenue-free grants and, if invalid, to annex them, was reserved. Under Regulations 19 and 37 of 1793, *Badshahi* grants (*i.e.*, direct from the Moghul Emperor) were recognized as valid, if the holder could prove his *sanad* and was in possession, and *Hukumi* grants (*i.e.*, from officials of the Emperor), though by their nature invalid, were accepted as valid if dated prior to 1765. No active steps, however, were taken to resume invalid grants until 1830, when a Special Commissioner was appointed under the provisions of Regulation 3 of 1828. The resumption proceedings then begun lasted for twenty years, and some thousands of estates were added to the revenue-roll.

Temporarily Settled Tracts.—The main temporarily-settled tracts in Bengal are the district of Darjeeling obtained from the Raja of Sikkim in 1835, and the Western Duars in Jalpaiguri, taken in 1864 from Bhutan, a large portion of the Chittagong district known as the Noabad area, and the Sundarbuns which comprises the southern portions of the districts of the 24-Parganas, Khulna and Backergunge. In addition to these, many scattered estates, which have become the property of Government by purchase at revenue sales or by alluvial accretions, are settled for terms fixed by Government.

Status of Zamindars.—The *zamindars* with whom the settlement was made, were a heterogeneous body of men differing as to historical origin and actual status. Some of them, like the Rajas of Tippera, Cooch Behar, Bishnupur and Birbhum, represented the old Hindu and Mahomedan Rajas of the country previous to the Moghul conquest by the EMPEROR AKBAR in 1576, or persons who claimed that status; others, like the Rajas of Rajshahi and Dinajpur, belonged to the great land-holding families that came into existence during the Mahomedan Government through its sufferance or favour, and were *de facto* rulers in their own estates or territories, and paid only a fixed tribute or land-tax ; while a third, the most numerous class, consisted of men whose families had held the office of revenue collector during one, two or more generations, and had thus, according to the practice of the East, established a kind of prescriptive right. Besides these, there were the revenue farmers who, since the grant of the *Dewani* in 1765, had collected the land revenue for the East India Company, and who also happened to be called *zamindars.* Thus, in 1790, the term *zamindar* included not only the mere collectors of revenue or tahsildars removable at pleasure, but also the landowners who held princely courts, dispensed justice in their own territories, maintained their own bodies of armed followers, and handed down their position from father to son. As a result of the Permanent Settlement, all these classes were placed on a uniform legal basis, and all previous differences in the customary *status* of several classes, which had grown out of differences in origin, were obliterated.

History of the Law of Landlord and Tenant.—Causes very similar to those that led to the feudalization of Europe were in force in India at the beginning and middle of the eighteenth century ; and, when the English found themselves masters of the country, they saw a state of things not unlike the feudal government of the Middle Ages. Consciously or unconsciously, Lord Cornwallis was thus led to introduce an imitation of the English system of landed property. The State assumed to itself and made over to the *zamindars* its own supposed proprietary right to the soil, as if the cultivators had no right to hold land against the will of the Government and its grantees. Deeper and closer observation, however, would have disclosed, underlying the upper layer, conditions of life and ideas of legal rights and obligations dissimilar to any with which Englishmen were familiar ; and they consequently failed to appreciate, far less to grapple with, them. The property in the soil was formally declared to be vested in the land-holders, but no adequate provision was made for the protection of the class of persons who were the real proprietors of the soil, and who deserved the largest amount of protection from the hands of Government.

Regulation 8 of 1793.—Regulation 8 of 1793, no doubt, imposed restrictions on the levying of any new *abwab* or *mathut, i.e.,* illegal cesses, from the ryots, and also made provision for the compulsory issue of *pattas,* or leases obtained *boná fide* from a landlord, and directed that they should not be cancelled except upon a general measurement of the *pargana* for the purpose of equalising and correcting the assessment, or upon proof that the *pattas* had been obtained in collusion, or that the rents, paid within the last three years, had been reduced below the *nirikband* of the pargana or pargana rate. But beyond these vague and general rules, there was nothing laid down to regulate the relations between the *zamindars* and the ryots. LORD CORNWALLIS was sanguine that the combined effects of the limitation and permanent settlement of the State demand and of the *Patta* regulations, would have the ultimate effect of adjusting the relations between the two parties. His hopes were, however, not realized. The first disappointment experienced was the failure of the attempt to enforce the issue of written leases for all tenancies. In many instances, the *zamindars* were unwilling to grant *pattas* or tendered them at more than the customary rates ; in others, the ryots refused to accept them either because they could not understand them, or because they thought the terms to be unfair; while the pargana rates, according to which, under Regulation 4 of 1794, the Civil Courts were to decide all disputes, varied from pargana to pargana and even in adjoining villages, and never were, nor could be, ascertained.

A constant struggle was thus kept up between the parties. The ryot refused to pay his rent, and the *zamindars* had no legal means of enforcing the payment from him with the same rigid punctuality with which the collector insisted upon the payment of the Government revenue. The result was a widespread default in the payment of the Government dues and the sale of a large number of estates. "By the end of the century," says a competent authority, "the greater portions of the estates of the Nadia, Rajshahi, Bishnupur, and Dinajpur Rajas had been alienated. The Burdwan estate was seriously crippled, and the Birbhum *zamindari* was completely ruined. A host of smaller *zamindaris* shared the same fate. In fact, it is scarcely too much to say, that, within the ten years that immediately followed the Permanent Settlement, a complete revolution took place in the constitution and ownership of the estates which formed the subject of that settlement."

Regulation 7 of 1799.—This circumstance caused the East India Company, which had to pay its dividends and to meet the expenses of the great war with Tipu Sultan, in which LORD WELLESLEY was then engaged, some alarm for the security of the revenue, and the Government, pressed by want of money, agreed to strengthen the hands of those on whom it immediately depended for its punctual payment. The notorious *Haftam*, or Regulation 7 of 1799, was, therefore, enacted "for enabling proprietors and farmers of land to realize their rents with greater punctuality." This Regulation gave the landlords practically unrestricted right of distraint. They were empowered "to distrain, without sending any notice to any Court of Justice or any public officer, the crops and products of the earth of every description, the grain, cattle, and all other personal property, whether found in the house or on the premises of any other person." To make matters worse, Magistrates were required to punish, by fine or imprisonment, ryots who could not establish the truthfulness of complaints of hardship brought by them against landlords, or their distraining agents, and the Civil Courts were directed to indemnify *zamindari* officers, or others employed in the collections, when improperly summoned. This Regulation was not meant to define or limit the actual "rights of any description of land-holders or tenants, which could properly be ascertained and determined by judicial investigation only, but merely to point out in what manner defaulting tenants should be proceeded against in the event of their not paying the rents justly due from them, leaving them to recover their rights, if infringed, with full costs and damages in the established courts of justice." "These last provisions," remarks MR. FIELD "scarcely required comment. There is scarcely a country in the civilized world in which a landlord is allowed to evict his tenant without having recourse to the regular tribunals; but the Bengal *zamindar* was deliberately told by the Legislature that he was at liberty to oust his tenants if the rents *claimed by him* were in arrear at the end of the year, leaving *them* to recover their rights, if infringed, by having recourse to those new and untried courts of justice, the failure in which might be punished with fine or imprisonment."

Regulation 5 of 1812.—There was, however, no intention to abrogate the rights of the ryots by Regulation 7 of 1799; and when, during LORD MINTO's administration, the evil effects of the Regulation became known, there was a strong revulsion of official feeling, which produced Regulation 5 of 1812 (the *Panjam*), whereby it was hoped to correct the bad effects of Regulation 7 of 1799. The preamble to this Regulation is somewhat in the nature of an indictment against *zamindars.* There were grounds, it was said, for believing that this class had abused their powers, and had been guilty of acts of oppression in connection with the distraint and sale of the property of their tenants. It was, therefore, enacted that *zamindars* were bound to serve their tenants with a written demand specifying the precise amount of their arrears, and, by way of relief or compensation, the tenant, if he disputed the justice of the demand, was enabled to get the attachment released by making a certain application within five days and binding himself to institute a civil suit to contest the distraint and attachment within another fifteen days. But this provision was clogged with formalities, and in practice, was inoperative. The defaulting tenant had to execute a bond with a surety before either a Commissioner, a Judge, a Collector, or the *Kazi* of the *pargana* that he would speedily institute his suit; and a civil suit, in those days involved much trouble, a good deal of time, and no inconsiderable outlay. If the suit was not instituted within the prescribed time, the attachment revived against the person and the property of the defaulter, who had given sureties for his action, and the property of the unfortunate surety, became liable for the arrears of rent, if no suit was brought. It is noticeable that there is raised in this law for the first time a doubt as to the existence of any regular standard known as the *pargana* rate. Failing such rates, rents were to be assessed and collections made according to the rates payable for lands of a similar description in the neighbourhood. There was another important section in the law by which an enchanced rate of rent could not be levied or awarded judicially unless it was preceded by a formal notice. Of the excellent intention of the framers of this law there can be no doubt, but it made no provision for defining rights by record, and thus only dealt with a part of the evil. It would, however, have been a relief, had it not been neutralized by other Regulations.

Regulation 11 of 1822.—In a despatch, dated the first of August 1822, the Government of India proposed to the Court of Directors to make a survey and record-of-rights of the permanently settled districts of Bengal, as being the only effectual means of defining and maintaining the rights of the ryots. This proposal was, however, never carried out; and, while the correspondence relating to it was proceeding, fresh legislation, which proved injurious to the ryots, was undertaken. A Regulation, No. 11, was passed in 1822, relating to the sale of land for arrears of revenue, which being, like the *Haftam*, intended to enable the *zamindars* to realize their rents and then discharge the Government revenue, really placed them in a position of abnormal superiority to their ryots.

Thus, up to the middle of the last century, the *zamindars* exercised an authority over the ryots far greater than that given to them by the original settlement of 1793. All legislation of this period, dealing with landlord and tenant, had one primary object, *viz.*, the security of the public revenue, and each successive Regulation served only to arm those who were under engagements for revenue with additional powers, so as to enable them to realize their demands in the first instance, whether right or wrong. "Under the *Haftam* process," as has been well observed, "the person of the ryot could be seized in default; under the *Panjam* process his property could be distrained; and in either case the proceedings commenced with what has been described as a strong presumption equivalent to a knock-down blow against the ryot." Remedies were no doubt provided in every Regulation for redress against any injustice by referring discontented parties to the Civil Court; but, constituted as the Civil Courts then were, the ryots were left without adequate means of relief for the most manifest extortions. Regulation 1 of 1793 had declared: "It being the duty of the ruling power to protect all classes of people and more particularly those who, from their situation, are helpless, the Governor-General in Council will, whenever he may deem it proper, enact such Regulations as he may think necessary for the protection and welfare of the dependent *taluqdars*, ryots and other cultivators of the soil," but no attempt even was made to give effect to this declaration till 1859.

Act 10 of 1859.—Act 10 of 1859, which may be described as the first modern tenant law, came at a time when the evils of the existing state of things were so patent that, in giving his assent to the Act as passed by the Legislative Council on the 29th of April 1859, LORD CANNING was able to say, "no objection is suggested to the nature of the settlement which the Bill contemplates." The Act defined the classes of tenants whose rent was fixed, and conferred a right of occupancy on those who had continuously held the same land for twelve years either personally or through their predecessors from whom the holding descended. This right of occupancy was of course conditional on the due payment of rent which could only be enhanced for certain specified reasons and by a certain procedure. The Act also made provisions for settling rent-disputes and questions of abatement and enhancement, renewed the attempt to bring about an interchange of *pattas* and *kabuliyats*, directed the delivery of receipts for rent, and transferred the original jurisdiction in suits between landlord and tenant from the Civil to the Revenue Courts. Distraint was modified but not abolished, and the registration of transfers of permanent transferable interests between the cultivator and the landlord was made compulsory. Act 10 of 1859 was amended by Bengal Act 8 of 1869, by which the trial of rent-suits was again transferred from the Revenue authorities to the Civil Courts.

Act 8 of 1885.—The principal defects of Act 10 of 1859 were that it placed the right of occupancy which it recognized in the tenant, and the right of enhancement which it recognized in the landlord, on a precarious footing. It gave, or professed to give, the ryot a right which he could not prove, and the landlord one which he could not enforce. The courts of law, with rigid impartiality, required the ryot to establish his occupancy right by showing that he had cultivated the same plot of land for twelve successive years, and demanded from the landlord the impossible proof that the value of the produce had increased in the same proportion in which he asked that his rent should be enhanced. The party upon whom lay the burden of proof was almost certain to fail. To this evil, the Bengal Tanancy Act (Act 8 of 1885) was intended to afford a remedy. The principle of the Act may be said to be based upon a system of fixity of tenure at judicial rents, and its three main objects are: first, to give the settled ryot the same security in his holding as he enjoyed under the old customary law; secondly, to ensure to the landlord a fair share of the increased value of the produce of the soil; and, thirdly, to lay down rules by which all disputed questions between landlord and tenant can be reduced to simple issues and decided upon equitable principles. A good example of the first will be found in the clause which throws upon the landlord the onus of disproving the ryot's claim to a right of occupancy; the second is illustrated by the section relating to price lists, which relieves the *zamindar* of the burden of showing that the value of the produce has increased; the third pervades the whole of the Act, and is specially conspicuous in the valuable section which authorizes an application to determine the incidents of a tenancy, and in the chapter which relates to records-of-right and settlements of rents. The maintenance of the principles of the Act is further safe-guarded by a section which restricts the power of entering into contracts in contravention of its fundamental provisions.

In pursuance of these main principles, the Act lays down rules to guide the courts in determining whether a tenant is a tenure-holder or a ryot; it provides a procedure for the registration of the transfers of tenures; it defines the position of ryots who hold at fixed rates of rent; it facilitates enhancement or reduction of rents of settled and other ryots by suit; it establishes a system for the commutation of rents payable in kind; it specifies the grounds on which a non-occupancy ryot may be ejected; it prescribes rules for instalments, receipts and interest upon arrears; it encourages the making of improvements, it restricts sub-letting, it provides for cases in which holdings are surrendered or abandoned, it protects the interests, both of the parties and of the general public, in cases of disputes between co-sharers, it lays down a procedure for recording the private lands of proprietors, it introduces a new system of distraint, it gives protection to sub-tenants when the interest of the superior holder is relinquished or sold in execution of a decree, and finally it provides for a survey and the preparation of a record-of-rights in respect of any local area, estate or tenure or part thereof, by a Revenue officer, and thus settles all disputes between landlord and tenant as to area, rent and status which are the chief subjects of contention. Moreover, by repeal of Act 8 (B. C.) of 1879, the Act under which settlements of land revenue were previously made by Governmnnt, the latter is placed on the same footing as other proprietors, except in regard to the retention of the certificate procedure for the speedy recovery of arrears of its rent. This is the existing tenant law of Bengal.

Thus the Legislature of 1885, nearly a century after the Permanent Settlement, settled the general principles by which the relation between the landlord and the tenant was to be regulated. Act 8 of 1885, though not professing to be an exhaustive code of the law of the landlord and tenant, is nevertheless a complete and self-contained enactment so far as the most important agrarian relations are concerned. Since it was passed in 1885, it has undergone various important amendments, but the principles on which the Act was founded have remained unaltered. The first amendment of the Act was made by Act 8 of 1886 which merely made some slight alterations in the sections dealing with the transfer of permanent tenures. It was followed by Act 1 of 1894 which made some changes in the procedure for the preparation of a record-of-rights under Chapter X.

Act 3 of 1898.—But the first important amendment was made by Act 3 of 1898 which completely recast Chapter X, dividing it into two separate portions, the first dealing with the preparation of a record-of-rights with a view to a settlement of the land revenue and providing for a settlement of fair and equitable rents for tenants of every class, as an integral part of the operations; and, the second, dealing with the preparation of a record-of-rights in areas where the land revenue is not being settled, the settlement officer being given power to settle fair and equitable rents only where application is made for such settlement by the landlord or tenant, and in other cases being confined to a record of the rent payable at the time the record-of-rights is being prepared. The Act also made some important alterations in the provisions relating to enhancement and reduction of rent.

Act I (B. C) of 1907. The last amending Act is Act 1 (B. C.) of 1907 (corresponding to Eastern Bengal and Assam Act 1 of 1908) which is probably the most important agrarian measure passed since 1885. This Act gives greater authority to the record-of-rights when duly prepared and published. The entry regarding rent has to be produced in all rent-suits and every entry in a record-of-rights is to be presumed by the Civil Courts to be correct until it is proved by evidence to be incorrect; and, a Court passing a decree at variance with entries in a record-of-rights has to record its reasons for so doing.

The Act also provides that, where a record-of-rights has been prepared and is being maintained, a landlord may apply to Government to have his arrears of rent recovered by the summary procedure prescribed in the Public Demands Recovery Act 1 (B. C.) of 1895. On the other hand, with the consent of the Governor-General in Council, a Revenue officer may be empowered to reduce rents which have been illegally enhanced above those entered as legally payable in a record-of-rights. The Act also lays down that no Revenue or Civil Court shall give effect to agreements or compromises between landlords and tenants, the terms of which, if embodied in a contract, could not be enforced under the Tenancy Act.

Record-of-rights.—(*a*) *Registration of estates*—A primary object of the framers of the Permanent Settlement was to record all rights in the land. Accordingly, the Legislature intended from the beginning that there should be at least one register kept up, showing the extent and particulars of each estate separately assessed with revenue payable to Government. The object was to enable the Collectors to apportion the revenue in cases of partitions, and to enable the Civil Courts to know when an estate changed hands, or happened to be transferred from one district to another.

Regulation 47 of 1793.—Regulation 47 of 1793 prescribed a general register of estates paying revenue immediately to Government. Each estate was to be described by name, and it was to be mentioned whether it consisted of a village, a *tappa* (group of villages), or a pargana. The nature of the grant was to be described and, if the estate had been partitioned, the shares were to be specified. A register of intermediate mutations was to be kept, and the general register was to be re-written every five years.

Act 7 of 1876.—The Registration Regulation of 1800 made further provisions and directed that the registers should be kept up by parganas, but, up till the passing of the Bengal Land Registration Act (7 of 1876), the law as to registration was not strictly enforced. Such registers as there were did not explain who the owners were, and furnished no information about under-tenures and ryots.

The present law requires the registration of all lands, whether revenue-paying or revenue-free, and every person in possession, as owner or manager of such lands, or of any share in such lands, is required within a certain period, and under heavy penalties, to register full particulars of the property in his possession. The object of the Act is not to make an inquisition into titles, but to identify all individuals on whom the Legislature has imposed certain duties and obligations in virtue of their being in possession of land as proprietors. The registers, required to be kept up now, are (i) a register A showing the revenue-paying lands in the district, (ii) a register B of revenue-free lands, (iii) a register C of lands paying revenue and those held revenue-free, arranged "*mauza-war*," and (iv) an intermediate register D for all kinds of land, showing the changes in proprietary rights and changes caused by the alteration of the district and other boundaries. These registers are now maintained in every district.

(*b*) *Registration of subordinate interests in land.* It will be observed that these registers do not profess to deal with any subordinate rights or interests. For several years after the Permanent Settlement, endeavours were made to maintain a record of these through *kanungos* and *patwaris*, but without success. An attempt was made to revive the system in 1885, but had to be abandoned. In 1895, the Land Records Maintenance Act was passed, and it has been worked experimentally in selected districts in Bihar, but the result has been disappointing. A scheme for the maintenance of records in the district of Chittagong was prepared in 1906-07, but it involved great initial expense and it has never been

7

carried into effect. The defect in the registration of subordinate interests has been partially supplied by the returns submitted under the Road Cess Act. The results are, however, vitiated by the system of summary valuation for the purposes of cess calculation which "withdraws from sight all details of tenures, under-tenures and raiyati holdings contained in such estates or tenures as are summarily valued." "In the instructions issued to the officers engaged in making re-valuations under Act 9 of 1880, an attempt was made to remedy this defect in the returns by declaring that the least possible recourse should be had to the process of summary valuation." The Bengal Tenancy Act (8 of 1885), however, now provides for the preparation of the record-of-rights of all interests in land. This has been prepared for the districts of Backergunge and Chittagong and for some portions of Midnapore, Tippera, Noakhali and Rangpur. In Faridpur and Jalpaiguri, a record-of-rights is approaching completion; in the rest of Midnapore, in Mymensingh, and Dacca and on both banks of the Brahmaputra and the Ganges it is in course of preparation, while arrangements have been made for its preparation in the district of Rajshahi. Another method of registering under-tenures is that under the Sale Law (Act 11 of 1859), which provides that they may be registered either in a common or a special register. Registration in the former protects them from being voided on sale of the estate for arrears, by any party other than Government, and registration in the latter protects them absolutely. Changes in certain subordinate interests, *viz.*, permanent tenures, and holdings at rents or rates of rent fixed in perpetuity (and shares of the same), are registered under the Bengal Tenancy Act. It will be clear that while the preparation of records-of-rights supplies completely the want of a register of all subordinate interests in land in the areas which they cover, no attempt has as yet been made to keep them up to date. In the areas which are not covered by records-of-rights, information as to subordinate interests is not only very defective, but is also available only in forms of which it is difficult to make use for administrative or statistical purposes.

Means of recovering revenue.—The revenue of the permanently-settled estates of Bengal is, as a rule, realized with great punctuality. As the *jama* was fixed by the Permanent Settlement never to be increased, so, on the other hand, remissions were declared to be inadmissible whether on the plea of loss from unfavourable seasons, inundations or any other cause. The payment of revenue is the first charge on an estate, and a default on the part of a *zamindar* renders his property liable to sale by auction for the realization of the arrears.

In the earlier years, the revenue instalments were payable monthly, and an arrear of revenue was defined to be "the whole or the portion of the *kist*, or instalment, payable in any month and remaining undischarged on the first of the following month." On the accrual of an arrear, the Collector was to serve a notice on the defaulter, and, on his failure to pay, had the option of putting him under confinement. The Board of Revenue alone, however, could direct the sale of the whole or any portion of the estate, and the sanction of the Governor-General in Council was in every case necessary. If the proceeds of the sale did not satisfy the Government demand, other properties of the defaulter might be sold to recover the remainder. In 1794 proprietors of land were declared to be no longer liable to be confined for arrears of public revenue, unless in the event of the whole of their lands having been sold without realizing sufficient to defray the amount due to Government. The Board were at the same time authorized to advertise estates for sale in anticipation of the sanction of the Governor-General, but no sale was to take place without such sanction.

Regulation 7 of 1799.—Material alterations were made in the law by Regulation 7 of 1799. It was then enacted that, when an arrear remained undischarged on the first day of the month succeeding that for which it was due, the Collector was immediately to require payment with interest, and if it were not then discharged, he was to proceed without delay to attach the estates of the defaulter, or such portions thereof as would be sufficient to make good the amount due. These estates were, however, not to be sold till the end of the year, and the Board were now for the first time authorized to sell them without any reference to the Governor-General. If the whole arrear was not recovered from the sale of the defaulter's lands, the deficiency was to be recoverable from any other property he might possess or by imprisonment of his person.

Regulation 18 of 1814.—By Regulation 18 of 1814 a further modification was made. It authorized the Collectors to advertise the lands of a defaulter for sale without the previous sanction of the Board of Revenue, if such lands constituted an entire estate or the whole of the defaulter's rights and interests in a joint estate. He was then to report to the Board, and was not to proceed to actual sale until receipt of the Board's sanction. This sanction the Board were empowered to give without any previous reference to the Governor-General in Council.

Regulation 11 of 1822.—The next Regulation of importance was 11 of 1822. During the twenty years which had elapsed since the passing of Regulation 7 of 1799, a great change had taken place. The object of the legislation of 1799 and the following years had been to secure the punctual realization of the revenue assessed at the time of the Permanent Settlement without resort to the old system of confining, and occasionally inflicting corporal punishment upon defaulters. The terror of personal coercion being removed, various devices had been practised to elude payment of the just dues of Government, and, in many instances, these dues had not been discharged, because those who were liable to Government for revenue were unable to compel similar punctuality in the payment of rent by their tenants. Armed, however, with powers for enforcing payment scarcely inferior to those exercised by Government for enforcing payments of its revenue, and taught by experience that persistence in fraudulent devices was sure to result in an ultimate loss, the great majority were successfully schooled to punctuality, and cases of default became yearly of less frequent occurrence. At the same time the prosperity, resulting from more than a quarter of a century's peace, largely raised the value of land, and, where arrears had been suffered to accrue, owing to temporary apathy, or mismanagement, or negligence, or dishonesty of agents, and, in consequence an estate had been brought to sale by the inexorable revenue authorities, flaws in their proceedings were eagerly searched for, and the Civil Courts were resorted to for setting aside sales at which irregularities had been discovered. The rights of the auction purchasers, not being very exactly defined by the Regulations, formed, moreover, a constant source of litigation. We find the Legislature in 1822, therefore, no longer devising means for bringing home their liability for arrears to proprietors, but improving the procedure of the revenue authorities, declaring what irregularities should be held material and what immaterial, and defining the exact interest acquired by purchasers at public sales.

Accordingly, Regulation 11 of 1822 dispensed with the necessity of issuing process of attachment before putting the estate up for sale; laid down the conditions necessary for the validity of the sale; defined the jurisdiction of the Civil Courts in cases of sale; framed rules for the conduct of sales; and vested the Board of Revenue with the power of annulling sales made by Collectors under their authority, not only in cases in which they appeared to have been irregularly conducted by those officers, but also in cases in which the defaulter might clearly appear to have been defrauded or deceived by his own agents, or in which the confirmation of the sale might, from any cause, appear to be a measure of excessive severity, or to be otherwise inexpedient or improper.

Regulation 7 of 1830.—The last of the Regulations concerned with recovery of arrears of revenue was Regulation 7 of 1830, which authorized Collectors to advertise estates in arrears for sale, and to proceed to actual sale without any previous reference for the sanction of the Commissioner, who had been appointed under the provisions of Regulation 1 of 1829, and to whom had been delegated some of the more immediate functions of the Board. No sale was, however, to be final until it had been confirmed by the Commissioner.

Act 12 of 1841.—This law lasted till 1841, when Act 12 replaced it. The provisions of the latter Act, which were re-enacted with slight modifications in Act 1 of 1845, are still to be found in almost their original form in Act 11 of 1859, the existing Sale Law for Bengal.

Act 11 of 1859.—Act 11 of 1859 was passed, not so much from any necessity for altering what had been done in 1841, or for remedying defects which time had brought to light in the working of the law as then settled, as from the expediency of affording protection to new interests which had sprung up during a further period of progress and prosperity. Under this Act an "arrear" accrues, if the *kist* or instalment of revenue of one month remains unpaid on the first of the following month, but in some cases notice for fifteen days before sale is required; persons, who have a lien upon any estate and who pay the money to protect such estate from sale, are allowed to add the amount so paid to the amount of the original lien ; sharers of a joint estate can protect their own shares from being sold for arrears along with the rest of the estate by applying to the Collector to be allowed to pay their share of the Government revenue separately. To guard against the accidental sale of their estates by reason of the neglect or fraud of their agents, recorded proprietors of estates are empowered to deposit with the Collector money or Government securities endorsed and made payable to the order of the Collector, at the same time signing an agreement pledging the same to Government by way of security for the revenue of the entire estate, and authorizing the Collector to apply them to the payment of any revenue that may become due therefrom ; and, lastly, to protect the holders of under-tenures from loss by the avoidance of their tenures by the sale of the estate, the law provides for two sets of Registers, one for Common Registry, and the other for Special Registry, Common Registry securing them against any auction-purchaser except Government, and Special Registry securing them against Government also. An appeal against a sale, held by the Collector, lies to the Commissioner, who may set aside the sale, if illegal, or, in cases of hardship, report to the Board, on whose recommendation it may be annulled by the Local Government. The Civil Courts have also been empowered to set aside sales in certain cases.

One feature of the Sale Law, which was early considered to be necessary, deserves notice. Soon after the Permanent Settlement it became a custom with the landlords to divest themselves of the trouble of management by farming out portions of their estates. There were so many encumbrances, that it was apprehended that, if they remained valid when the landlord's interest was sold for arrears of revenue, the prices realized would not be sufficient to meet the demands of Government. It was, accordingly, enacted in the Regulation of 1793, that, on a sale for arrears of revenue, all engagements subsisting between the proprietors and their dependent talukdars, farmers and ryots, on account of such land, should, with certain exceptions, stand cancelled. But this wholesale avoidance of contracts, made by the defaulting landlords, was soon recognized to be excessive, and successive Regulations and Acts have mitigated the terms.

Interests protected under Act 11 of 1859.—The protected interests under the present Sale Law are :—

(1) *Istimrari* or *Mukarrari* tenures, which have been held at a fixed rent from the time of the Permanent Settlement ;

(2) Tenures, existing at the time of the Settlement, which have not been held at a fixed rent; provided that the rents of such tenures shall be liable to enhancement under any law, for the time being in force, for the enhancement of the rent of such tenures ;

(3) *Talukdari* and other similar tenures created since the time of the Settlement and held immediately by the proprietors of estates, and farms for terms of years so held, when such tenures and farms have been duly registered under the provision of this Act; and,

(4) Leases of lands whereon dwelling-houses, manufactories, or other permanent buildings have been erected, or whereon gardens, plantations, tanks, wells, canals, places of worship, or burning or burying grounds have been made, or wherein mines have been sunk.

It is to be remembered, however, that the protection that this law affords to the tenure-holders and the check it introduces on attempts by *zamindars* to utilize it as a means for enhancing rents, are much lessened through the period of limitation laid down by Section 2 of Act 3 (B. C.) of 1862.

General account of tenures, under-tenures and holdings in Bengal.—At the Permanent Settlement, Government, by abdicating its position as exclusive possessor of the soil, and contenting itself with a permanent rent-charge on the land, escaped thence-forward the labour and risks attendant upon detailed *mofassal* management. The *zamindars* of Bengal Proper were not slow to follow the example set them, and immediately began to dispose of their *zamindaris* in a similar manner. Permanent tenures, known as *Patni* tenures, were created in large numbers, and extensive tracts were leased out on long terms. By the year 1819, permanent alienations of the kind described had been so extensively effected, that they were formally legalized by Regulation 8 of that year, and means were afforded to the *zamindar* of recovering arrears of rent from his *patnidars*, almost identical with those by which the demands of Government were enforced against himself. The practice of granting such tenures has steadily continued, until at the present day a large proportion of the whole permanently-settled area has passed from the direct possession of the *zamindars*. In these alienations the *zamindars* have made far better terms for themselves than the Government was able to make for itself in 1793. It has rarely happened that a *patni*, or even a lease for a term of years, has been given otherwise than on payment of a bonus, which has discounted the contingency of many years' increased rents. It is a system by which, in its adoption by the *zamindars*, their posterity suffers, because it is clear that if the bonus were not exacted, a higher rental could be permanently obtained from the land. This consideration has not, however, had much practical weight with the land-holders. If a gradual accession to the wealth and influence of sub-proprietors be a desirable thing in the interest of the community, then the action of the land-holding class is not in this instance a subject for regret.

MADRAS

Based on the Administration Report of Madras, 1911-12.

Early Settlements under the British Government.—The first general acquisition of territory by the East India Company—the first from a revenue point of view—was the country round Madras, which now forms the Chingleput district. The revenue of this tract was assigned by the NAWAB of the CARNATIC as a contribution towards the expenses of the wars undertaken in his behalf. At first the direct administration was not assumed; the revenues were collected on the native plan; in 1780, however, the country was leased out by the Company in large farms on nine-year leases. The renters failed and the estates were sequestered in 1788. The district was then placed in charge of one or two Collectors, as the chief revenue officers were called, the term being borrowed from Bengal. The most famous of these, MR. LIONEL PLACE, determined to restore the ancient village organization as the basis of revenue management and settled the amount of the government revenue with the village councils, leaving it to the villagers to assess themselves individually. This system might have succeeded, but was summarily terminated in 1802. Under the orders of the Court of Directors the district was then divided into estates, each estate being assessed at a fixed sum varying according to its size and resources, and these estates were sold by auction to the highest bidder. The next acquisitions of the Company in point of time were the Northern Circars (administrative divisions) five in number, which form the present districts of Ganjam, Vizagapatam, Godavari, Kistna and Guntur in the north-east of the Presidency. They were obtained by grant from the Delhi EMPEROR in 1765 and came at once under British administration. It was found that they consisted of large farms held by large renters called *zamindars* (as in Bengal), or, in a few cases, by native chiefs whose titles dated from the pre-Mahomedan period, and of crown lands (Havēli lands) reserved for the support of the Governors of the province or members of the royal family and their immediate dependents. The *zamindars* were left in possession and the crown lands were parcelled out and leased to revenue farmers for a term of years. In 1769, provincial councils were formed after the model of Bengal to supervise the revenue management. They found the work of looking after the *zamindaris* too great for them and did not effect much. The next step was the appointment by the Court of Directors of a Special Commission or Committee of Circuit to make tours in the districts and institute inquiries into rights and interests. Their instructions were conceived in a liberal and enlightened spirit, but the local councils did not support the members and the renters did all in their power to thwart them. The Commission therefore resulted in failure. In 1786 a Board of Revenue was established in Madras on the pattern of the Board already existing in Bengal, and about the same time individual Collectors took the place of provincial councils in the Circars. In the same year that the Madras Government entered on the management of the Northern Circars, the Bengal Government assumed that of Bengal, Behar and Orissa, and experiments were conducted in the latter case in very much the same way as in the former. The Bengal Government, however, came earlier to a decision, and when LORD CORNWALLIS arrived in India in 1786 the plan of the permanent settlement with the Bengal *zamindars* had already been arranged. A tentative settlement of the whole of Bengal for a period of ten years was announced in 1789, and in 1792 the experiment of a permanent settlement was declared to be confirmed. Pressure was brought to bear on Madras by the Bengal Government to adopt the same policy and the Court of Directors sent out orders to this effect in 1795. The Madras Board, however, replied that it was hardly prepared to recommend the perpetuation of the settlement and required time for the collection of further information. In 1799 positive orders were issued from England that LORD CORNWALLIS' permanent system was to be adopted throughout the Madras Presidency. Eventually the Madras Government reported to the Supreme Government that it was possessed of materials for a permanent zamindari settlement in certain parts of the country. A special commission was appointed, and between the years 1802 and 1804 the northern districts of Madras were permanently assessed. The lands already in the hands of *zamindars* were confirmed to them in perpetuity, the assessment (*peshkash*) being fixed at two-thirds of half the gross produce estimated on an average of the previous thirteen years. That is to say, half the produce was to be left to the cultivator, one-sixth was to be the *zamindar's* share, and the remainder, two-sixths, was the Government revenue. The amount of the latter once fixed was unalterable, no increase ever being leviable on account of extension of cultivation to waste lands. The crown lands were parcelled out into estates of a convenient size assessed in a similar manner and sold as permanently-settled revenue farms to the highest auction-bidder. In course of time, however, many of these artificially created estates came back to the hands of Government owing to failure of the purchasers, and the lands then became subject to the ordinary (temporary) settlement, there being none to repurchase them. Though great numbers of *zamindaris* were sold for arrears, purchasers were generally found for them and they did not cease to be permanently-settled estates. Only in a comparatively few cases was there no purchaser, and then the lands were retained by Government as *Khas Mahals, i.e.*, estates retained in the hands of Government. While these measures for the settlement of the more ancient territories of the Company were in progress, new territories were added to the Presidency and the question of land assessment came up again for discussion in connection with the part of the country ceded to the English in the south.

In 1792 the first war with TIPU SULTAN of Mysore placed a considerable tract of country comprising the present districts of Salem, part of Madura, and Malabar in the hands of the British. The second war with TIPU added Canara and Coimbatore. According to a treaty with the NIZAM OF HAIDARABAD in 1800, what are now called the Ceded Districts, viz., Bellary, Anantapur, Kurnool and Cuddapah, were ceded in perpetuity. In 1801 all the remaining possessions of the NAWAB of ARCOT, in the Carnatic comprising the present districts of Nellore, North and South Arcot, Chittoor (excepting a portion), Madura, Ramnad, Trichinopoly and Tinnevelly were made over to the British, thus carrying their possessions down to Cape Comorin. The state of Tanjore had been brought under British management in 1799 owing to the incapacity of its Hindu ruler. In the territory thus newly acquired, the same distinction was found as in the Northern Circars. That is to say, there were lands held by numerous chieftains (*poligars*) and lands held direct from Government.

CAPTAIN READ AND SIR THOMAS MUNRO'S SETTLEMENT.

The village-lease system, 1798.—The general idea was to make a permanent settlement, but with whom was not determined. CAPTAIN READ's instructions, were to grant leases to the headmen or the chief inhabitants of each village, that is to say, one or more individuals were to be selected to hold the settlement and to pay, according to the terms of the lease, the amount that might be agreed upon as the revenue of the village. The leases were to be annual at first, but after sufficient information had been gathered, it was hoped that leases might be made for periods of five years. To begin with, READ offered terms to the headmen of single villages or groups of villages based on the recorded assessment of HAIDAR's reign corrected by comparison with accounts of actual cultivation. At the same time the interest of the cultivator was guarded and a detailed field survey was made. This led to the idea of assessing each field according to its quality and leaving the cultivator free to keep the field or relinquish it and take another. The survey was finished and the assessment on each field determined by the year 1798, and a proclamation was made setting forth the terms of the settlement, one of the conditions being that all the resident cultivators of a village should be jointly responsible for the revenue due on all the lands cultivated during the year.

Extension of Permanent Settlement, 1803-1805—This was not the kind of 'village-lease' which the Board had intended, and an explanation was called for. Meanwhile READ was called away to the second Mysore war, and the consideration of what had been done was suspended by the attempt to carry out the orders to introduce the permanent settlement. In accordance with the orders received in 1799, the Baramahal was divided in the years 1803-1805 into numerous revenue farms which were sold by auction to the highest bidder. A great many of the farmers, however, failed in the second year after having *pillaged* the villages in their farms, and many estates fell into the possession of Government again. It became evident that the permanent settlement could not be carried out, and a return was made to READ's system, which was in fact a ryotwari settlement, *i.e.*, a settlement with each individual cultivator (ryot). The estates held by a few of the *poligars* in the Ceded districts and in the Carnatic districts were permanently settled, but in the majority of instances the *poligars* attempted to resist the British authorities in the hope of continuing the same lawless course of exactions and plunder that they had adopted before the annexation and were therefore destroyed or dispossessed.

Reversion to village-lease system, 1808.—The attempt to create artificial estates, which were to be assigned in perpetuity subject to the payment of a fixed sum as *peshkash* or land-revenue, was a general failure, and at last it became apparent that the conditions of by far the greater part of the Presidency were unsuited to the introduction of the *zamindari* system. In 1808 the Government of Fort St. George determined to recur to the system of 'village-leases' in the districts in which the permanent settlement had not been established, and in which settlements were made with the individual cultivators and the revenue collected from them by Government servants on the principles worked out by READ, MUNRO and the men who had served under them. The chief objects of the change of system appear to have been economy and a desire to introduce a plan of settlement approximating to the *zamindari* settlement in perpetuity. Under the village-lease system the settlement was to be made with the village headman or with the general body of villagers, or, failing them, with a renter. The revenue due to Government was to be assessed on the average of the amount collected from the village in previous years. The leases were to be for triennial periods; they were afterwards made decennial. The great difference between this system and the *ryotwari* system was that, under the latter the cultivators were at liberty to extend or curtail their holdings and were only responsible for the payment of the revenue assessed on the fields actually held by them; under the former the lessee had no power of relinquishing any portion of his holding during the currency of the lease. It was not a successful experiment on the whole. The most general cause of failure was over-assessment. Lessees could not be found for many villages, and in these the *ryotwari* system was continued.

Introduction of the ryotwari system, 1817.—One great advantage of the *ryotwari* system was the opportunity it afforded of acquiring information respecting revenue matters, of ascertaining the dues of Government and the rights of the cultivators. The universal introduction of the *zamindari* system had been held in abeyance for fear of sacrificing the interests of Government in the then imperfect state of knowledge, and the *ryotwari* system was discontinued in favour of the village-lease system before all the benefits it was capable of yielding had been realized.

However, in 1817 the Court of Directors issued instructions for the abolition of the village-leases and the re-introduction of the *ryotwari* system wherever practicable. In 1820 MUNRO become Governor of the Madras Presidency and took his seat in time to preside over the final establisment of the ryotwari system. The early *ryotwari* settlements had many defects. Restrictions were placed upon the relinquishment of land, and heavy assessments were imposed on garden lands, *i.e.*, lands cultivated with special crops. The survey and settlement were conducted so rapidly that there were very great inequalities. The assessments were largely dependent not so much on the estimates of produce as on former assessments which had been run up to a high pitch under the Mysore Government or the Nawab, as the case might be. Such rates were liable to become unbearable when the selling price of grain became very low as it did for a number of years. Hence various devices were resorted to in order to mitigate the burden. All this has now given way to careful survey and deliberately-framed and carefully-equalized assessments. Garden lands have been classified and assessed as dry lands in all districts except Malabar and South Canara, in which districts, owing to peculiar conditions of garden cultivation, it has been found necessary to assess gardens at special rates.

Ryotwari Settlement.—Before proceeding to describe the machinery by which the existing settlements have been effected, the modern meaning attached to the term *ryotwari settlement* may be explained. It means the division of all arable land whether cultivated or not into 'fields' and the assessment of each 'field' or group of fields at a fixed rate for a term of years. The 'field' is an arbitrary area. Where a survey-field comprises the holdings of two or more occupants it is sub-divided where such holdings are separately identifiable. Survey-fields may also be sub-divided to distinguish portions transferred or relinquished. Sub-divisions are surveyed and marked on the field maps but not demarcated on the ground. The occupant pays the revenue so assessed on the area he actually occupies. This area may be constant, or may be varied from year to year by the relinquishment of old fields and the taking up of new. The occupant deals directly with the Government and is responsible for no one's revenue but his own. He is given a document called a *patta,* which sets forth the extent and assessment of each survey-field or sub-division thereof in his occupation. This *patta* is liable to revision every year so as to bring it into accord with the actual state of affairs. The occupant thus enjoys all the advantages of proprietorship, subject only to the payment of the revenue due on the lands held during the year. The lands can be inherited, sold or burdened for debt in precisely the same manner as a proprietary right, provided that the person in whose name the land is registered in the Government accounts pays the revenue due to the State. The average area of each holding is a little over 6 acres.

Institution of the Settlement Department, 1855.—The Government determined in 1855 that a general revision of assessments should be made throughout the Presidency, founded on an accurate survey and a more or less exact classification of soils which seemed the only right basis of a land-revenue settlement. The Government of India and the Home Government concurred in the necessity of the measure, and the Revenue Settlement Department was constituted in 1858. The Settlement Department at first undertook to demarcate the village and field boundaries. This was a tedious process involving much arbitration and the investigation of many disputes. The marks erected in many cases were temporary and destructible, and had frequently to be renewed by others of a more permanent nature. This unsatisfactory work continued to occupy much time and attention, until the demarcation of boundaries was made over to the Survey Department in 1864. The results of certain operations of the department were not, in the opinion of Government, satisfactory. Its organization as a separate department, distinct from the local revenue establishments, was held to be defective, and the experience and knowledge of the district officers were lost, their interest not being enlisted. Government accordingly resolved to place all settlement operations under the immediate supervision of District Officers controlled by the Board of Revenue. The new system was introduced in two districts—Tinnevelly and Nellore. But in Nellore the experiment resulted in such a failure that in 1868 Government transferred the settlement back to the special department on the ground that the retention of the special department was the only method by which it was possible to ensure celerity and efficiency in settlement work, consistency and uniformity in the details of re-assessment and a fair measure of relative equality in the resulting taxation, and to save the country from the neglect which must occur if the Collector and subordinate revenue officers were withdrawn from their ordinary duties. Settlement operations continued everywhere, except in Tinnevelly, under the control of the special department till the end of 1873, when, on the transfer of the then Director to the Board of Revenue, that appointment was placed in abeyance for some months. But in the following year decision was given in favour of the continuance of the department under a separate head.

The department continued to be so administered till the latter part of 1879, when, in consequence of financial exigencies, the appointment of Director was abolished, and the strength of the department reduced by about half. The department, under these altered conditions, was, administered by a member of the Board of Revenue.

This arrangement lasted till the end of 1882, when the appointment of Director was revived and conjoined with that of the newly constituted Directorship of Agriculture.

But at the reorganization of the Board of Revenue in April 1887, the department was again placed under the direct charge of the Board, one of its members assuming the portfolio under the designation of the Commissioner of Revenue Settlement and Director of Land Records and Agriculture. In 1903 the Survey Department was placed under the Commissioner of Revenue Settlement and his designation was changed into Commissioner oi Revenue Settlement, Survey, Land Records and Agriculture.

Original Scheme of Survey and Settlement.—The scheme of survey and settlement as originally sketched out is shown under the following fourteen heads: (1) a revenue survey showing all the principal variations in the surface of the soil as hills, jungles, roads, channels, tanks, topes, houses, cultivated and cultivable lands, and also exhibiting accurately the sizes of the fields in these last two classes of land ; (2) the minimum size of fields was to be one acre of wet, and two acres of dry land ; interstitial holdings were to be treated as sub-divisions of such fields ; (3) permanent boundary marks were to be established, and, field, village and taluk maps prepared ; (4) assessment was to be *ryotwar ;* (5) the terms of the annual settlement made with each ryot were to vary simply with the area and quality of the lands held by the ryot, and his use or non-use of water from a Government source ; (6) soils were to be divided into a few classes based on real, tangible differences of composition ; (7) the settlement officer was to estimate, as nearly as possible, the productive power of the land, stated in quantities of some one of the ordinary grain crops—paddy for irrigated lands, and *cumbu, cholam* or some other grain for unirrigated ; these estimates (grain outturns) were to form the basis of the ultimate assessment ; they were to be carefully made on such a scale as would allow for indifferent crops and bad seasons ; (8) the land was then to be valued with regard to nearness of village roads, markets, irrigation facilities, etc., and the field or village was to be classed accordingly ; (9) the assessment was to be moderate ; existing rates were generally based on 50 per cent. of the gross produce for wet, and 33 per cent. for dry, lands ; SIR THOMAS MUNRO's maximum was 30 per cent., and this was now adopted on the assumption that the average assessment would be about 25 per cent. of the gross produce ; (10) the ryots' payment was to vary every 7 or 10 years with the commutation price of the standard crop to be calculated on the average of the prices prevailing during the previous 7 or 10 years ; (11) it was believed that it would not be found necessary to divide the country for the purpose of official scales of prices, *i.e.*, one scale was to apply to the entire Presidency for the term adopted; but this principle was abandoned in practice, and the commutation prices for each district have been calculated independently; (12) the grain outturns were to be unalterable for a period of 50 years; (13) it was to be open to the ryot to compound for a fixed annual payment for a term of years; and (14) the Survey Department and the Settlement Department were to be separate, the former under a Surveyor-General, the latter under a Superintendent of Settlement.

Subsequent Modifications.—Objections taken subsequently with regard to certain detailed points were decided at different times as enumerated below: (1) the restriction as to the size of fields has been removed; the maximum was once fixed at 2 acres for wet and 4 for dry land; but now, as a rule, each revenue-field (*i.e.*, each parcel of land on which previously a separate assessment is fixed) will form a survey-field; in exceptional cases two or more revenue-fields may be clubbed together subject to the following conditions:—(*a*) every survey-field so formed must consist of entire revenue-fields; (*b*) no survey-fields so united should exceed 6 acres of wet or 12 acres of dry land; (*c*) the revenue-fields forming a survey-field should be held on the same tenure; *inam* and *ryotwari* land should not be taken together; (*d*) no existing revenue-field need be divided, however large; (2) the assessment was to be made on the net produce, *i.e.*, after deducting the expenses of cultivation and a percentage for vicissitudes of season, unprofitable areas, etc.; in 1864, the Government share of the net produce was fixed by the Secretary of State at one-half; (3) the term of settlement was to be 30 years, *i.e.*, both grain outturns and commutation prices were to remain unalterable for that period; subsequently it was decided that at each settlement or re-settlement of a district Government would fix at their discretion the period for which such settlement or re-settlement should be in force, and on the expiry of that period Government would revise the assessment, in such manner as might then seem just and proper, either with reference solely to a rise or fall in, prices, or with reference also to other considerations such as would require a re-classification of soils or a re-calculation of the grain outturns; (4) leases for a term of years at reduced rents were found to be unnecessary for the encouragement of large holdings; (5) another important question which came up for disposal at the time of the initial settlement of the districts of Godavari, Kistna and Guntur was the method to be adopted in assessing the additional amount to be paid, over and above the land assessment, for water supplied from Government irrigation sources such as the Godavari and Kistna canals; in these districts it was decided to impose a uniform charge of Rs. 4 per acre for irrigation supplied for a single crop, in addition to the land assessment, which was determined as if the land was unirrigated; it was desired to adopt a similar plan in all other districts where it was found practicable; as a matter of fact, however, the only other district in which the system has been introduced is Kurnool, in some parts of which irrigation is supplied from a canal which was originally worked by the Madras Irrigation Canal Company under a guarantee from Government, and the principle was maintained when the Company's works were taken over by Government; the land-assessments were fixed without reference to the facilities for irrigation; in districts subsequently settled, the assessment on irrigated lands was determined by a consideration of the value of the paddy (rice) crop grown on the best irrigated land, gradations of rates being formed to meet the conditions of inferior qualities of soil or defects in the sufficiency or regularity of the water-supply; this system of consolidated wet assessment was extended to the irrigated lands under the Godavari, Kistna and Kurnool-Cuddapah canals at the re-settlements of those districts; (6) formerly it was the practice to charge the rates settled for irrigated lands, on lands irrigated by wells, where such wells were situated within a distance of ten yards of a Government source of irrigation, although Government had incurred no expense in sinking the wells; the justification for this course was that the wells derived their water-supply by percolation from the Government source. Under recent orders, however, such lands are no longer assessed as irrigated, and the cultivator is allowed to enjoy the benefit of irrigation from his well free of any additional charge.

Preliminary Investigation.—In the first instance it is necessary to obtain a general view of the characteristics of the district. Particulars of the climate, rainfall and physical features of such tracts or divisions as differ from each other distinctly have to be ascertained; information relative to its past history, its years of plenty or famine, its land tenures, mode of taxation, and the causes of gradual progress has to be obtained from the Collector's records; the relative values of such sources of irrigation as the various tracts possess have to be estimated; a general idea of the prevailing soils must be acquired; at the same time, information is gathered as to how different tracts are affected by roads, canals, markets, towns, hill ranges or seaboard; the methods of cultivation pursued, the crops grown, the mode of disposal of surplus grain, the markets mostly frequented and the wages paid to labourers have to be inquired into. A district is for administrative purposes, divided into taluks; each taluk has to be visited and the revenue officers and leading cultivators consulted.

Classification of soils.—The next step is to classify the soil. At first the number of sorts in a class was only two, but experience proved such a scale to be too inelastic, and the number was increased first to three and then to five, *viz.*, best, good, ordinary, inferior, worst. In determining the classification, the soil is turned up to the depth of about 9 inches. The classification of each field is noted on the village map and in a register. It is usually found that soils run in considerable blocks round which a line can be drawn on the map. Inside the block small differences in a few scattered fields are disregarded to avoid multiplying blocks.

Classification of fields.—A revenue system based on field assessment seems to demand naturally and necessarily the separate classification of each individual field, and this is the sanctioned method of the department; it is, at the same time, laid down that though the details of classification extend to each field, the wider comparative view of the operations should never be lost sight of, as it is most desirable that the land should be viewed in a comprehensive way by the classifier.

Grain outturn.—The next stage is to ascertain what amount of crop each different class and sort of soil will produce. The same kind of crop is not always grown on the same soil, nor on the same field, from year to year. It is necessary, therefore, to choose one or more standard grains (always food-grains, as food-products are the ultimate standards of values) to represent the general or average produce. The crop most extensively grown on irrigated lands is paddy (rice); on unirrigated (or dry) lands several varieties of food-grains are grown; and the crop cultivated on the largest area according to the cultivation accounts is usually selected as the standard, or more often two crops are taken, the areas under other crops being for settlement purposes presumed to be cultivated with one or other of these according to the relative value of the crop. A fair average outturn of the standard grains is then ascertained per acre of each class and sort of soil;

and this is called the grain outturn. The criterion of such outturns is experience, and this is sought in experiments by officers of the Settlement and Agricultural departments, in the knowledge acquired during long years of service by Tahsildars and similar responsible officers of Government, in the records of produce entered in the old village accounts, and in the admissions of the ryots. The actual experiments consist in reaping, threshing and measuring the crop upon small areas in selected fields. The number of experiments in some districts has exceeded two or even three thousand.

The results are taken as a general guide to the grain outturns and no more. The experimental reapings (or *kails* as they were called), however, are now to a great extent given up, and general inquiries and statistics already collected are relied on instead.

Commutation price.—The grain outturns are next commuted into money. The commutation price is fixed on an average struck on the prices of a long series of years, so as to ensure that the advantages of good, and losses of bad, years may be balanced, and to preclude all risk of the Government share of the produce being sold to the ryot at a price which he cannot always command; and a percentage allowance (formerly 10 and now generally 15 per cent.) is made for cartage of grain to markets and for merchants' profits. For all the earlier settlements, the average taken was based on the prices of the 20 years from 1845 to 1864. But since 1885 the period has, under the orders of Government, been altered into the twenty non-famine years immediately preceding each settlement. From the results obtained by applying the commutation rate a deduction of from one-sixteenth* to one-fourth is usually allowed on account of vicissitudes of season, and in view of the fact that the survey areas of

* One-twentieth is allowed in the case of lands under first-class sources of irrigation in Nellore.

fields include small extents of uncultivated land, such as field-ridges, irrigation distributaries, etc.

Cost of cultivation.—Against the average value of the produce thus determined has to be set off the 'cost of cultivation,' the estimation of which is one of the most difficult of the various steps in connection with a settlement. The items of cost usually included in the estimate are (1) ploughing cattle, (2) agricultural implements, (3) seed, (4) manure, and (5) labour required for ploughing, sowing, reaping, etc. The method of calculation varies according to the description of crops grown, and the method of cultivation, as well as according to the mode in which these items are paid in each district. In some, payments are made in grain, in others in money, and in some in both grain and money. The payments made in grain are converted into money at the commutation price adopted for the settlement. The cost of bullocks and of the implements of husbandry is distributed over the number of years during which they are estimated to be serviceable, and the other items are calculated for each year. Calculations are first made for the area which can be cultivated with one plough and one pair of bullocks, and the required calculations for an acre are deduced from them. The usual practice is to work out the expenses for the best soil, and then to diminish this standard proportionately according to the quality of soil. This method is open to objection on the ground that the cost of cultivating poor soils is greater if a maximum yield is sought therefrom than for superior soils. But it is to be borne in mind that the cultivator is content with a much smaller relative outturn from inferior soils, and omits many processes such as repeated ploughings, manuring, weeding, and hoeing, which are resorted to on more fertile lands. Now, the expenses of cultivation are taken to be thes ame as has been already determined in neighbouring settled districts. These expenses being deducted from the gross assets, *i.e.*, the value of the total outturn, the result is the approximate net produce of the land under examination, and half of this, or more often rather less than half, is taken as the Government demand. The 'straw' is usually taken as a set off against the item 'feed of bullocks.'

Assessment.—The principle has always been that the assessment is to be moderate. The old rates were generally based on 50 per cent. of the gross produce for wet, and 33 per cent. for dry, land. When revision began, the maximum was reduced to 30 per cent., the average assessment being about 25 per cent. But in the course of time a gross-produce percentage was not considered sufficiently accurate. Net produce was to be ascertained by deducting the cost of cultivation, etc., as explained in the last paragraph, and in 1864 the Government share or revenue was fixed at half the duly ascertained net produce. Recent calculations have shown that the ryotwari revenue actually collected at the present time is less than 10 per cent. of the gross produce.

Increment remissions.—In introducing the new rates the ryots are granted "increment remissions" in cases where the new assessment is greater than the old beyond a certain percentage; if the increase in individual cases exceeds 25 per cent. of the old assessment, the old assessment *plus* 25 per cent. of that assessment will be levied in the first year and the remainder remitted. If the full amount of the new assessment cannot be reached by the twelfth year, the balance remaining after levying 25 per cent. in the first year will be levied in equal instalments in the succeeding eleven years. Increases of Rs. 3 and less will be levied in the first year whatever the percentage may be.

The Settlement Register.—The *Settlement Register* is the foundation on which the whole revenue administration rests. It forms a complete 'Domesday book' recording accurate information regarding every separate holding, large or small. The area of each field is given in acres and cents or hundredths of an acre, and the assessment thereon is noted against it. A single field on the survey map may actually be divided amongst twenty ryots. In such a case there will be twenty sub-divisions, and each ryot will have a separate sub-line in the register giving full particulars of his *holding*, even though the extent of it be no more than one-hundredth part of an acre. From the register is prepared a ledger known as the *chitta* which gives each ryot's personal account with Government. Every field or fraction of a field held by the same ryot is picked out from the settlement register, and entered in this ledger under his name with particulars of the area, assessment and other details. The total of the areas shows the extent of his different holdings in the village, and the total of the assessments is the amount due thereon by him to Government. A copy of this, his personal account, is given to each ryot with a note as to the date on which each instalment falls due and is known as his *patta*. An English descriptive memoir giving full details touching each village and its settlement, and an account of all lands held tax-free or on favourable tenure is also printed. A sketch map of the village showing the tanks and channels, and all similarly assessed fields laid out into blocks is attached to it. The descriptive memoirs of all the villages in each taluk consecutively numbered are bound into one or more volumes with their respective sketches and thus supply complete information regarding every village.

Pattas.—The introduction of settlement is effected by the issue of *pattas* to those entitled to them, and this is one of the most important parts of the process of settlement. In the districts first settled, it was thought snfficient to issue *pattas* in the names of persons entered iu the accounts as they then stood, but latterly, more has been done and many thousands of *pattas* have, after due inquiry, and where no civil disputes arise, been changed from the names of deceased ryots or vendors to those of the actual occupants of the lands exhibited in them.

Jamabandi.—The duration of the settlements and re-settlements hitherto carried out is 30 years. During that period, neither the grain outturns nor the commutation rates are altered. But, as under the ryotwari system, each cultivator is free to hold or relinquish whatever fields of his holding he likes, or to take up other available fields, and, as, deductions are sometimes made from his total assessment, there must be an annnal settling up to show what lands each ryot has actually held, and what amount, on all accounts, he has actually to pay for the year; his *patta* may be revised or he may, if necessary, be given a fresh *patta* every year. This process, which is called the annual settlement or *jamabandi*, is conducted not by the special department but by the ordinary revenue staff. In this way the information recorded in the settlement registers is periodically corrected, so that when the existing settlement expires and revision becomes requisite, it will in general, merely be necessary to determine what the revised rates of assessment shall be, and to substitute these for the existing rates entered in the village accounts.

Re-settlement.—Initial settlements having been carried out in all districts throughout the Presidency, the operations to be carried out in the future will be almost entirely re-settlements. A re-settlement consists in a revision of the rates of assesment which were calculated not on holdings but on fields which may now be in the same or in different holdings. In revising these rates, changes in prices, in means of communication, in the accessibility of markets and in the quality of the irrigation sources since the original settlement, are taken into consideration, together with any other indications of economic progress or retrogression. And, as a rule, the rates are raised or lowered all round in defined tracts by the same percentage. A re-settlement may also be made by remodelling the original settlement by a re-classification of soils and the application of a new set of money rates based on a fresh calculation of grain outturns, cultivation expenses etc.

The Remission Rules.—From what has been said above, it will be seen that, in the various calculations made in fixing the final money rates on each field, allowances are made for seasonal failure and various other agricultural risks. As a matter of policy, however, remissions either total or partial of these rates are granted, as a matter of grace, under executive instructions in cases of loss of crop. Such remissions have occasionally been allowed to cure mistakes in assessmeut, which the utmost care cannot always prevent; but relief on this ground is rarely required since Government are always ready and willing to correct, after a settlement has been introduced, any error which, in particular instances, may have led to over-assessment. The circumstances which render the grant of remissions expedient are the frequency of droughts or of immoderate rain, the enormous number of petty holdings, the improvidence of a large proportion of the cultivating class, and the undesirability of keeping arrears hanging over their heads for a series of years. Owing to the multiplicity of holdings and the general numerical weakness of the revenue staff, enquiry into individual losses is often impracticable; and relief can usually be rendered only where the loss of crop can be readily located, estimated and verified: and it is essential that it should reach the ryot. These considerations have been kept in view in the rules actually issued from time to time. In the case of "wet" land, which is of comparatively limited area and productive of comparatively valuable crops, total failure of the crop over the plots registered in the accounts and demarcated on the ground as separate fields, or sub-divisions is a fact readily ascertained and verified: and the rules empower the Collector to remit the assessment in such cases in all years. In the case of failure, total or partial, of crops on "dry" land and the case of partial failure in "wet" land, whether this takes the form of an indifferent yield over a whole field or of a total failure of crop in parts of a whole field, the loss in particular fields is not only difficult to ascertain but its determination by subordinate officials is not susceptible of any satisfactory check. To meet these cases, therefore, an allowance is made at settlement in reduction of the assessment which practically meets the losses of all but exceptionally unfavourable seasons. To provide for the calamities of exceptionally bad years the rules allow of a proportionate remission of assessment uniform over tracts where the crops have suffered in a marked degree. The remission rules as stated above are executive instructions, liable to be altered from time to time at the pleasure of the Government.

Character of Land Tenures.

The following are the main varieties of land tenures under the Government:—(i) perpetual free-holds held under a title-deed showing proprietorship as against the Government, and paying no land revenue; (ii) enfranchised *inams*, or grants of land or of the land revenue thereon, held under a title-deed showing proprietorship as against the Government, and paying a quit-rent fixed for ever, calculated at a favourable rate; (iii) *zamindaris*, or landed estates held under a *sanad* or title-deed showing proprietorship as against the Government, and paying a land revenue or *peshkash* fixed in perpetuity; (iv) unsettled *palayams*, or landed estates held without *sanads*, the land revenue on which may be raised at the pleasure of the Government; (v) individual holdings under what is termed *ryotwari tenure* without a *sanad* expressly declaring proprietorship, and paying a revenue subject to additions and deductions in certain special circumstances and subject to revision at intervals of thirty years; (vi) *inam* holdings including *jagirs*, or grants of land or of land revenue, held under a tenure dependent on the fulfilment of certain conditions; (vii) land held on special conditions as (*a*) on improvement leases called *cowles*, and (*b*) under the favourable rules for planting *topes* or groves of trees.

Perpetual Freeholds.—The perpetual freeholds now existing were created under the rules for the redemption of land revenue and quit-rent on enfranchised *inams* under the rules in force during the latter half of the nineteenth century. Under these rules the redemption of land revenue was permitted in the case of (i) sites of buildings (ii) gardens of limited extent attached thereto, and (iii) hill plantations of exotic products, such as tea, coffee, cinchona, etc. The rate of redemption was first fixed at twenty-five times the annual land revenue; but, in 1895, it was raised to twenty-nine times such sum. In *zamindaris* the registered zamindar alone was given the right to redeem the land revenue. In the case of ryotwari lands, the ryot holding directly from the Government alone had the right. On payment of the redemption money in full, with the cost of survey and demarcation, the party redeeming the revenue was furnished with a title-deed. The redemption of quit-rent on enfranchised *inams* introduces the question of the *inam* tenures of this Presidency; but it is only necessary here to mention that inamdars holding lands enfranchised from service, or from resumption by Government, but subject nevertheless to a quit-rent, were allowed until recently to redeem that quit-rent in perpetuity. In the case of the *inam* title-deeds issued before the 28th February 1895, the sum payable for the redemption of quit-rent was fixed at twenty times the amount, but in the deeds issued after that date, it was stipulated that the quit-rent should be redeemed by thirty years' purchase. Having regard to the disadvantages arising from the capitalization of the State's annual revenue from land, Government decided in 1896 that the redemption of land-revenue should be disallowed except in cases in which they had already pledged themselves to allow it. No absolute free-holds can therefore be now newly acquired in this Presidency. The holders of free-holds have unlimited powers of alienation. The free-hold is absolute against that demand of the Government only which represents the Government's right to share the produce, and gives no immunity from other Government demands, such as for irrigation, roads, sanitation, education and so forth; in all of which cases the land may be subjected to separate cesses or demands. The redemption in no way affects sub-tenures, rights of occupancy, or other similar rights; and the freedom conferred is absolute only against the Government.

Inams enfranchised, but unredeemed.—Holders of enfranchised *inams*, who at the time of enfranchisement were granted the option of redeeming at any time the quit-rent payable on their lands, but have not availed themselves of the concession, have full power of alienation and pay quit-rent; but such quit-rent is not liable to periodical revision.

Zamindaris.—In the case of *zamindaris*, the land has been assigned in perpetuity with a proprietary title as against the Government. The land revenue, technically called "*peshkash*", is a charge on the land. Zamindars hold under a deed termed a "*sanad-i-milkeut istimrar*" and give in exchange a corresponding *kabuliyat*, or acceptance. Act 2 of 1904 declares certain estates to be impartible and also inalienable beyond the life-time of their proprietors except in circumstances which entitle the managing member of a joint Hindu family, not being the father or grandfather of the other co-parceners, to make an alienation of the joint property binding on the shares of the other co-parceners independently of their consent. The alienation of an impartible estate beyond the life-time of its proprietor for the payment of land-revenue due to Government is also prohibited unless the written consent of the Collector of the district in which the estate is situated is first obtained. In the case of *zamindaris* not brought within the scope of the Act, the proprietors are at liberty to transfer, without the previous consent of the Government, their right in the whole or part, however small, of their *zamindaris* to any person they please by sale, gift or otherwise; and such transfers are to be held valid and to be respected by the courts and officers of Government, provided that they are not repugnant to the Mahomedan or Hindu law, or to the regulations of the British Government. In order to be valid against the Government, and in order to liberate the transferer from his liability to pay Government dues, such transactions must be first registered in the Collector's office; and, where the alienation is of a sub-division of the estate, the *peshkash* on the sub-divided portion must be determined by the Collector. The Government do not regulate the succession to *zamindaris*. The position of the cultivators in *zamindari* estates had not been clearly laid down under Act 8 of 1865. Generally the cultivators had occupancy rights and were bound to pay only rent to the landholder. Occupancy rights were, however, gradually trenched upon, and in some estates claims were set up inconsistent with such rights. Fresh legislation thus became necessary. An Act (the Estates Land Act) was passed in 1908 repealing the provisions of Act 8 of 1865 and laying down the substantive rights of the land-holders and the tenants, and the procedure to be adopted in the collection of rents. The land being permanently settled, that is to say, the land revenue on it being fixed for ever, extension of cultivation brings no increase of revenue to the State. The fact that the zamindar has to pay a permanently-fixed revenue does not exempt him from liability to general, local and municipal taxes.

Palayams or unsettled estates.—The *palayams* for which no sanads have been granted are called unsettled *palayams*. The important difference between unsettled *palayams* and *zamindaris* is that, in the case of the former the Government have the power to resume the grant at pleasure or to alter or revise the conditions on which it is held, as for example by revising the amount of revenue paid by the holder.

Ryotwari Tenure.—The ryotwari system of holding under the Government has now been the principal tenure of this Presidency for over three-quarters of a century. The *pattadar* or registered holder of land under the ryotwari system is, as regards Government, the responsible proprietor of the land entered against his name in the land register of the village, until it passes from his possession by sale for arrears of revenue, or in some other legal manner. A registered *pattadar* may, so far as Government is concerned, alienate, in any manner he pleases, the whole or portion of his holding, provided (i) that unless and until such alienation is registered in the village records, the alienor remains liable for the revenue and all other legal charges due on the land, just as if no such alienation had occurred, and (ii) that when the alienation is registered the alienee takes the land subject to payment of any arrears of assessment or other legal charges due on it, and to the same obligations as those under which it was held by the alienor. If a registered *pattadar* improves his holding by constructing a tank on it, or digging a well, he is not chargeable with any additional assessment for such improvements but he is not entitled to claim, as of right, any reduction of assessment on account of space occupied by the work. He is bound to pay the assessment fixed on his field or holding, whether cultivated, waste or fallow, in the prescribed instalments, unless it be remitted. The registered *pattadar* is entitled to work minerals on his land, but is liable to pay therefor a separate assessment in addition to the assessment above referred to which is for surface cultivation.

Ordinary Inam Tenures of Land.—When the State has given up its right to the land revenue, or a portion of it, in favour of an individual or an institution, or to remunerate persons for performing certain duties, the grant is termed an *inam* or *manyam*. In 1858 a Commission was established to examine the titles of the possessors of *inams*, and of the inams that were confirmed, to continue those that were still required for religious charitable or village service and to enfranchise those of other descriptions, if the possessors wished by commuting for a moderate quit-rent the right of the Government to prevent alienation, to resume, or to demand service. Service inams are held revenue-free or subject to favourable rates. They cannot be alienated without forfeiture of the favourable tenure. The conditious of the grant must in each case be observed by the holder and the Government claim an absolute right to adjudicate as to the proper fulfilment of those conditions. In the case of village service *inams*, the holders are bound to perform certain administrative duties, and are styled village officers: the succession to these inams is governed by a special enactment, and is hereditary in most districts. The *inams* attached to the more important village offices have, however, been enfranchised, and the village officers are now remunerated by money salaries.

Land held on Cowles, etc.—A *cowle* is a grant of land free of assessment for a certain period, or subject to favourable assessment gradually rising to full assessment. Until the full assessment is imposed, the holder is subject to the terms of the contract contained in the *cowle*. The *cowle* tenure is usually granted to induce ryots to bring under cultivation unpromising waste lands, or to plant trees or shrubs for green manure. Lands held under the tope rules are of the same nature, their object being to encourage tree planting. The terms of a *cowle* reserve to Government the power of re-entry on breach of its conditions.

Mirasi Rights.—These rights are not sufficiently strong to be classed as tenures or rights against the Government, such as zamindari or ryotwari; but they are sometimes more than the mere preferential right to occupy new land, and they are recognised by the Government. The only trace that remains now of the special rights of the old communal oligarchies is the claim by certain hereditary *mirasi-dars* in Chingleput district to fees upon waste land which may hereafter be brought under cultivation, and upon lands now occupied which may hereafter be relinquished and again re-occupied. These fees were formerly taken from the gross produce before the division of the crop, and were then paid to the *mirasi-dars* both by the ryots and by the Government. They are now made payable entirely by the ryots, liberal allowance having been made for them in arriving at the rates of assessment charged on their lands. The fee payable by the ryot under these circumstances is a yearly sum of two annas in each rupee of the Government assessment, this amount being held to represent the old average rate of 3 per cent. of the gross produce of the year. The right to collect these fees is recorded by the Government in the land revenue registers, but their collection is left to the *mirasi-dars* themselves. The total amount of these fees payable to *mirasi-dars* in Chingleput district is very small, but the right is tenaciously maintained, and represents what was in former days a highly important institution.

Unassigned Lands.—Unassigned land within a Government ryotwari village is either the assessed or unassessed. The unassigned land of a village is at the disposal of the Government. Subject to the instructions of the government officers, certain portions are reserved for the gratuitous communal use of the villagers, as tanks, streets, channels, threshing-floor, burial-grounds, cattle-stands, etc., while in all villages, except on the West Coast, a house-site and a backyard, with permission to cultivate garden produce in it free of all assessment, are provided gratuitously for each family. The addition to, or subtraction from, the area of viliage-site is provided for by fixed rules. Unassessed waste lands of a village, which are not yet assigned, and are not reserved for these or other special purposes, are available to ryots for cultivation.

Unassigned lands outside the recognised limits of any village are insignificant on the plains, which are fully occupied by the village communities, but they abound on the hill ranges where the indigenous tribes have established only a very partial occupation. Special rules have therefore been framed for the sale of waste lands on the Nilgiris (except in seven villages, six of which have been transferred from the Coimbatore district), on the Palnis outside the Kodaikanal Settlement in the Madura district, on the Shevaroy, Kollimalai and Yelagiri hills in the Salem district and on the Kollimalais in the Trichinopoly district. In the Nilgiris, excluding the Nilgiri-Wynaad, no assessment is charged till the sixth year on forest or grass land newly taken up under these rules and planted with coffee, tea, cinchona, rubber or other special products. Similar lands in the Niligiri-Wynaad are allowed to be held free of assessment for three complete years.

Tenures other than those under the Government.—In a ryotwari country the most important considerations connected with land tenures are those which concern the relations of the Government with persons holding immediately from it. The system of tenancy under such land-holders is, however, fully developed, registered ryots sub-letting their lands and living on the difference between the rents they obtain and the assessment they pay to the Government. In the districts on the East Coast, lands are generally rented out by the land-holders either for a fixed annual payment in money, or for a share in the produce. Ordinarily dry and garden lands are rented for money and irrigated lands for a share in the produce. In the case of permanently settled estates every ryot in possession of ryoti land, not being old waste, is the owner of the occupancy right in the land in his holding.

There are other tenures of a special nature in South Canara and Malabar, which need not be described here.

BOMBAY

System of Survey and Settlement.

Characteristic of the System..—The Bombay system of survey and settlement is what is known as a *ryotwari* system: that is to say, the land assesment is placed, not as in the Bengal system, upon the large estate under the single landlord, or as in the United Provinces upon the village as a whole, but upon the separate holdings of individual ryots—a characteristic which it shares in common with the Madras system alone.

The present system was not introduced until the year 1835; but a brief summary of the previous Revenue history is necessary as an introduction to that of the new system.

Early British System.—The early British system of land assessment was derived from the Mahrattas, according to which the revenue for the year was fixed annually for each village as a whole in accordance with the character of the season. The distribution of this amount over the individual holdings was left to the custom of the villager, the result being a crop of different systems bewildering in their extraordinary variety. Generally speaking however the land assessment was divided into two parts, *viz.*, the land assessment proper, usually a cash rate fixed upon the local land measure which also varied indefinitely, and extra assessments called *Pattis* which were determined at the pleasure of the local officers and ordinarily consisted of commutations in cash for demands originally made in kind. In addition to these there were house taxes, cattle taxes, trade taxes, transit taxes and a number of others, varying according to local custom.

The first attempt of the British in the field of Land Revenue administration upon these lines was, it must be admitted, a total failure, and the condition of the agricultural population during the first 10 years of British rule went from bad to worse. The main causes of this failure were :

(1) The natural inexperience of the first British administrators in dealing with a highly complicated and—to them—unintelligible system.

(2) The sudden fall in prices due to the decrease in the demand for grain owing to the break-up of the Mahratta camps and court coupled with a large increase in the supply owing to the return of the Mahratta soldiery to agricultural pursuits.

(3) The corruption of the native staff owing to the heritage of the 'farming system' of Baji Rao, the last Peshwa, which made 'common honesty not respected in any mamlatdar.'

The result was a condition of great over-assessment which necessitated a system of annual remissions, which, again, however did not benefit the ryot, as the remissions meant for him merely went into the pockets of the Revenue subordinates, and thus only served to aggravate the evil conditions which they were meant to cure.

Mr. Pringle's Settlement, 1827.—Experienced officers saw that the only remedy was the introduction of a proper system of survey and assessment based upon fixed principles and the abolition of all the anomalies and cnnfusion inherent in the old system. In 1827 therefore Mr. Pringle of the Civil Service was deputed to devise such a system for the Poona and surrounding districts. His settlement attempted to fix the government demand at about half (55 per cent.) the net produce, and therefore entailed not only estimates of the yield of various crops and soils, but of the cost of cultivation. But owing to the continuous fall in the money value of agricultural produce, due to a variety of circumstances, which need not here be specified, and the consequent yearly increasing pressure of the state demand, the settlement was found to press heavily on the people.

The execution of the different operations of Mr. Pringle's survey was entrusted entirely to native agency without either the experience or integrity needed for the task, and at a subsequent period the results obtained were found to be nearly worthless. The preliminary work of measurement was grossly faulty, and the estimates of produce, which formed such an important element in the determination of the assessment and which had been prepared in the most elaborate manner, were so erroneous as to be worse than worthless. But meanwhile the settlement had been introduced, and with the result of aggravating the evils it had been designed to remove. From the outset it was found impossible to collect anything approaching to the full revenue. In some districts not one-half could be realised. Things now went rapidly from bad to worse. Every year brought its addition to the accumulated arrears of revenue, and with them the necessity for remissions or modifications of rates. The state of confusion in the accounts, engendered by these expedients, was taken advantage of by the native officials to levy contributions for themselves.

Introduction of the New System, 1835.—It was when matters had reached this crisis that, at the end of 1835, an examination and correction of the operations of Mr. Pringle's survey in the Indapur taluka of the Poona Collectorate were ordered in view to a revision of the settlement in that district. The duty of conducting the work was entrusted to Mr. Goldsmid of the Civil Service, then an Assistant Collector, and Lieutenant Wingate of the Engineers. With these gentlemen Lieutenant Nash, of the Engineers, was subsequently associated. This was the real commencement of the revenue survey in the Bombay Presidency.

As the new operations progressed, the extremely defective character of the original survey became apparent. Much of the measurement had to be undertaken *de novo*, but when areas were not faulty to any great extent they were accepted as the basis of the new assessment. An entirely new method of classification was adopted. Abandoning all attempts to arrive at a theoretical ideal of assessment by endeavouring to discover the yield of indifferent soils, and assigning a certain proportion of this as the government demand, the survey officers adopted the purely practical principle of relying upon their own judgment as to what the soil *could* pay and arranging their assessments accordingly. With this object soils were divided into 9 classes based primarily upon their depth and quality of texture, and by a process of field 'classification' which comprised an examination of the soil of each field for depth and quality, all the fields within the talukas were assigned to one of these classes.

An assessment rate was then assigned to each soil class 'by visiting fields of each of the nine kinds of soil, and determining with the assistance of those best skilled in agricnlture and by the knowledge and judgment they themselves possessed, what assessment, after taking into consideration the uncertainity of rain and all other circumstances, an acre of each sort of soil could bear, and applying rates thus fixed to returns, prepared and checked with the greatest care, of the quantity of soil of each sort existing in each field.'

The assessment so determined was then guaranteed for thirty years, the cultivator being absolutely secured against any additional assessment on account of any improvements he might make to his holding during its currency.

The system was frankly empirical, but the results showed the wisdom of the course taken. In the second year of the Indapur Settlement, the Revenue Commissioner reported to government that "*the sum actually collected has never been so great* except during the first four years of our occupation, when, it is generally acknowledged, our demands were much too high"; and, again, "the outstanding balances *have never yet been so low at the end of the official year as they were last year.*" A marked extension of cultivation was one of the immediate results of the settlement, nearly 68,000 acres of waste land having been brought under the plough by the end of the second year, besides more than 3,000 acres reclaimed by immigrants from other districts, attracted to Indapur by the revived prosperity of the taluka.

Extension of Survey operations into other districts.—The Indapur experiment having proved thus signally successful, the survey operations were rapidly extended to other districts, the same results following everywhere. In the course of a few years separate surveys were organized for the Poona and Ahmednagar collectorates and for the southern Mahratta country. As experience was gained, improvements were introduced in the methods of procedure, the end in view always being to render them as simple and susceptible of thorough check and control as possible, as well as to adapt them to the varying circumstances of the districts which successively came under the survey. The main improvements so introduced were :—

(*a*) the improvement of survey methods and the gradual evolution of an accurate village map;

(*b*) the permanent demarcation of the fields by official boundary marks (usually large earthern mounds) at the corners by which the survey was stereotyped;

(*c*) improvements in the details of field 'classification' and particularly the evolution of systems of classification for application to irrigated lands, such as land watered from wells, tanks or dams, and rice lands by LIEUTENANT DAVIDSON and MR. FRAZER TYTLER.

(*d*) improvements in methods of assessment by the collection of large bodies of statistics and closer inquiry into agricultural conditions.

The Joint Report, 1847.—But it was not till 1847 that a definite and permanent form was given to the system of survey operations. In that year, in accordance with the orders of government, the superintendents of the three surveys met at Poona, and drew up a Joint Report setting forth what they considered to be "the best means for bringing the somewhat diversified operations of the several revenue surveys of the Presidency into conformity as far as practicable, and also for ensuring the results of the surveys being turned to the best account, and maintained in their original integrity in the future management of the districts." The Superintendents, besides defining the objects of a revenue survey, and the general principles on which the assessment of land should, in their opinion, be conducted, submitted a body of rules for definition and demarcation of fields, the settlement of boundary disputes, the classification of soils, the interior regulation of surveys and the administration of settlements, which, having received the approval of government, became an authoritative Manual for the conduct of all future survey operations. Up to this period, though there had been a general adherence to the main principles by which the work was governed from its beginning, some diversity of practice had prevailed in the different surveys. A greater degree of uniformity and completeness was now given to it.

Further extension of the Survey, 1854.—In 1854 the new survey was extended to the Gujarat and Konkan districts and was slowly extended over the whole Presidency till the last taluka Devgad of Ratnagiri was brought under its operation in 1891. Long before that time, however, the first surveyed talukas fell in for the revision of their assessment on the expiration of the period of

30 years' guarantee, beginning with Indapur in 1868. From that time original and revision settlements proceeded *pari passu.* Each class of settlement has its own peculiar features, but in a general review of this kind it will be sufficient to describe the system as a whole, touching on individual peculiarities wherever necessary.

The System of Settlement.—The system as a whole requires to be treated under three heads, *viz.*, (*a*) Survey, (*b*) Classification and (*c*) Assessment.

(*a*) *Survey.*—Under this head the most important point for consideration is as to the 'unit of assessment' The unit adopted, at the outset at any rate, was the survey number based upon the theoretical principle of a field capable of being cultivated by one pair of oxen. When the survey was first started, no attempt was made to indicate holdings belonging to different persons, but after a time a practice arose of demarcating sub-divisions of survey numbers in accordance with the rights of private persons in the land, and clubbing two or more of these sub-divisions (which in Survey parlance were known as *pot* numbers) together so as to form one survey number. The practice, however, led to the entry in the revenue accounts of a large number of minute holdings, and for the convenience of revenue administration it was considered necessary to check it. Accordingly, in 1868 orders were issued by Government directing that sub-divisions below a certain limit (which varied in different tracts and different classes of land) should not be recognized, except with the special sanction of the Survey Commissioner, and these orders remained in force until the passing of Bombay Act 4 of 1913. The result was that at present the survey number became a unit for mapping and account purposes only, and there existed many rights in the land included in a survey number which it was not attempted to show on the map or in the village accounts. In fact registration in the village accounts was evidence of liability for assessment but not necessarily of proprietary or other rights in the land.

There thus arose two classes of title to land : one depending upon Registration in the Revenue Accounts as the holder of one of the official sub-divisions of land, survey number or pot-number, and the other upon proprietary title such as would be recognised by the courts. Very often the two would of course coincide, e.g. when the occupant of the land was both the actual owner and also the individual whose name was recorded in the revenue records. Still more often, however, the nominal and practical occupants would be different, as there was no obligation on a cultivator who had, for example, sold either the whole or part of his land to get the new occupant's name entered in the Revenue Records which would not in any case have recognised the subdivision of his lands effected by sale of a share. Hence arose a curious distinction between what may be called the 'registered' and the 'possessory' title to land which remained till it was abolished by Bombay Act 4 of 1903.

Act 4 of 1913.—The abolition of this anomaly was ultimately due to the passing of the Record-of-Rights Act, Bombay 4 of 1903. For administrative purposes it was found essential to have a record of the proprietary and other rights in the land, and under the provisions of this Act a register called the Record-of-rights was introduced in all the agricultural districts of the Presidency. This register was at first intended to be purely statistical, but in course of time, thanks to the revelation of actual conditions which was the result of its introduction, the absurdity of keeping up the old fictional system of a registered, apart from a possessory, title to land became increasingly obvious. By Act 4 of 1903, therefore, the Land Revenue Code of 1879 was amended, the old 'registered' title to land abolished and the Record-of Rights made the foundation of the occupancy system of the Presidency, by being converted into a record not only of possession, but also of liability for the payment of land revenue.

At the same time, as a natural corollary to this change, the survey number or *pot* number ceased to be the unit of assessment and holding, and for them was substituted the 'sub-division of a survey number' held by the possessory occupant and noted in the Record-of-Rights.

(*b*) *Classification.*—The object of the system of 'classification' was to discover the relative values of fields and to express that value in terms of a scale, so that when a 'maximum rate' of assessment was framed for lands of the highest class the rates for the subordinate classes could at once be worked out proportionately ; this was the general object of the system and it is one that can easily be understood. In its detailed aspect, however, the 'classification' system is extraordinarily intricate, partly owing to the exigencies of local conditions, and partly to the idiosyncracies of the different survey officers whose hands moulded it into shape. The main features of the system, however, are as follows :—

(1) Lands were divided into 'classes' such as dry crop and irrigated ; the latter again being subdivided into sub-classes, such as garden lands (i.e. lands watered from wells, dams etc.) and rice lands.

(2) For each of these classes the various 'factors' which go to make up their fertility value were distinguished. Thus, in the case of dry crop the main factor of value is the soil : in irrigated lands it is the soil and also the water supply, whether natural or artificial.

(3) For each of these 'factors' a scale was arranged according to which its relative value could be assessed. Thus, in the case of the 'soil' factor the scale ordinarily employed was the familiar Indian scale of 16 annas. This was divided into 10 classes—16 annas, 14, 12, 10, 8, 6, 4½, 3, 2 and 1 anna. By a procsss of careful examination of

the whole field its soil could be placed in one of these classes and its value thereby fixed relatively to the value of the best or 16 anna class of soil. Similarly for the other 'factors' different kinds of scales were arranged by which their value relative to the best class could be discovered for any particular field. Thus to take the case of tank-irrigated rice land, the factors are three in number, viz. soil, drainage from higher ground and facility of irrigation from the tank. For each of these factors there was a scale in which the value of the factor for the field could be calculated, the result of the three calculations taken together giving the value of the whole field relative to the best field of the same 'class.'

It is the variety of factors recognised in different parts of the survey, the different kind of scales arranged and the methods by which they were combined which makes the 'classification' system so intricate. But, through all the variations the object was one and the same, viz., to find and express the values of fields of each 'class' relatively to that of other fields within the same class.

(c) *Assessment*—At the original settlements the method of giving the rates of assessment adopted was that known in the Punjab as 'aggregate to detail', *i.e.* a lump sum was fixed for the whole settlement area usually a 'taluka' which was then distributed over the individual fields comprised therein. The 'aggregate' was determined by general considerations such as the past revenue history of the tract, the area under occupation, the incidence of the assessment and the ease with which it was paid, and the general condition of the population. By a study of statistics gathered for each of these heads the settlement officer could determine whether the existing aggregate was fair or not and make his proposals accordingly.

This aggregate was then distributed over the survey fields through the medium of 'maximum acre rates' fixed for the various 'classes' of lands. These rates were applied to the best classes of lands and the rates for the inferior classes derived proportionately in accordance with their position in the classification scale. In order to allow for variation in conditions between different parts of the area under settlement, it was divided into homogeneous 'groups' of villages, comprising those similarly situated with regard to rainfall and communications, and the general pitch of the rates was varied as between group and group to allow for their respective advantages or disadvantages.

The rates fixed in this manner were usually guaranteed for 30 years at the end of which period they were revised. The main principles upon which the revision was conducted were the same as those followed at the original settlements, viz., the settlement officer, after a study of the history of the taluka during the past 30 years, decided whether the rates could be raised or whether they could be kept at the same level or even required to be reduced. He would then make his proposals for the next 30 years accordingly. The result of these proposals was ordinarily an increase in the assessment as the rates at the original settlements had usually been kept low designedly and were consequently much below what government had a right to demand. It was found, however, that hardship was caused if the rates were raised above a certain percentage; hence rules were laid down limiting the enhancement over an individual taluka, village or holding to 33%, 66% and 100% respectively. Rules were also passed allowing increases to be levied not at once but by instalments of 4 annas, 8 annas and 12 annas in the rupee at intervals of 2 or 3 years.

Another important question which has always been anxiously debated at revision settlements is that of the taxation of improvements. During the currency of the original settlement the ryot was guaranteed against any increase of assessment on account of improvements made to his holding at his own expense. Instances of such improvement would be the conversion of dry-crop land into garden or rice land, or the cultivation of land classed as uncultivable. When the time for revision came, however, the question arose as to the policy to be adopted in regard to such improved lands. On the one hand, from the strictly legal point of view they were undoubtedly liable to the full assessment, but on the other hand, government wished to adopt a liberal policy with a view to encouraging the introduction of such improvements by every means in their power. It would take too long to describe the various measures by which this policy was made effectual, but the result is that the ryot is now at liberty to make any improvement to his holding, secure in the knowledge that no extra assessment whatever will be levied on that account in future.

Suspensions and Remissions—The rates fixed are legally leviable in full whatever the character of the season, the justification being that the survey assessment is fixed as an average of good and bad years, and that consequently the cultivator can save enough in a good year to pay the whole assessment in a bad year. Experience, however, showed that among the smaller land-holders and in tracts subject to frequent vicissitudes of season this idea was fallacious, and in 1906-07 a regular system of suspensions and remissions was introduced. The system authorizes the Collector, when he has ascertained by local inquiries that, owing to a partial or total failure or destruction of crops throughout any tracts, suspension of the collection of land revenue is necessary, to grant suspensions according to a scale to all occupants, agriculturists and non-agriculturists alike, without inquiry into the circumstances of individuals. As regards remissions, the grant of them depends on the character of three seasons following that in which the assessment is suspended. Ordinarily, suspended arrears which are more than three years old are to be remitted by the Collector. The remissions are to be granted to occupants cultivating their own holdings, and also to non-cultivating occupants, provided that when land is cultivated by tenant, remission is granted by the superior holder or landlord to the inferior holder or tenant.

Main features of the system.—The following extract from a Government Resolution well sums up the main features of the system just described:—"At the time when the existing system was introduced, that is to say, about sixty years ago, government were still confronted with the formidable problem of settling upon an equitable and workable basis the revenue demand for a vast number of small holdings. Several modes of settlement, based on pre-existing practice, had been tried; some of them, such as the PRINGLE settlement, had disastrously failed. Out of the prevailing confusion the principles of the existing system of survey settlement were evolved by the genius of MESSRS. WINGATE and GOLDSMID, the authors of the celebrated Joint Report. Upon the principles laid down in that report has been founded a system of land tenure and assessment admirably adapted to the requirements of the widely varying conditions of the different parts of the Presidency. Under the system of measurement and classification by subordinate agency, subject to the test of technically trained and skilled supervising officers, methods were employed by which the area of every one of these small holdings could be measured, and the relative productive capacity of the soil estimated with scientific accuracy. By the system of grouping, the relative economic and climatic advantages of different tracts were duly taken into account. In this manner the equitable distribution of the assessment was secured. The rates charged at the original settlement per acre of land occupied were, in many instances, extraordinarily low as compared with those previously levied. But as anticipated by the framers of the system the effect of the fixed tenure and of a certain and moderate assessment was at once seen in a rapid expansion of cultivation, which even at the low rates of assessment sanctioned yielded a large increase of revenue. The extensive areas of waste land existing at the time when the system was introduced have been employed largely for the growth of crops valuable for export purposes. Despite the check occasioned by many bad seasons and several disastrous famines, and notwithstanding the heavy burden of indebtedness with which the agricultural population was saddled from the first, the value of land and the prosperity of the country, and with them the revenue, have steadily increased. When the first leases of thirty years expired, it was found possible to increase the assessment by very substantial amounts; but the enhancements have, with rare exceptions, been borne without difficulty. The survey department has cost the state from first to last many lakhs of rupees. But the outlay has been repaid over and over again. One peculiar merit of the system deserves mention. By the division of the whole culturable area into what may be called units of assessment, the extension of cultivation was made to carry with it an increase of revenue, while the revenue-payer was placed in a position to ease his burden by giving up the occupation of lands unprofitable to him. The extensions of cultivation which have occurred have thus been profitable to the state no less than to the individual, whereas under a *zamindari* or kindred system, the state would have gained nothing, however much cultivation had extended throughout the whole of 30 years' leases. But it has not been only as a revenue-producing instrument that the survey department has proved its usefulness. The system to which the valuation of soils has been reduced is in many respects unique, and has resulted in a record of that valuation complete for innumerable small parcels of land. Probably no other province or country is possessed of any similar record. Its chief and immediate value for administrative purposes is that it enables field operations to be entirely dispensed with in all future settlements. The change of assessment can be decided for a whole tract on a review of its economic conditions and revenue history, and the people are saved from all the uncertainty and harassment consequent upon inquiry into the circumstances of individual holdings. The greatest credit attaches to the founders of this system, which has stood the test of experience and practical application in the most satisfactory manner. Developments have been introduced, but in no particular have the principles, and in very few have even the individual rules and directions laid down in the Joint Report, been widely departed from."

Tenures.

The tenures of the Bombay Presidency may be divided into 3 classes *viz.*, the survey tenure, inam tenures and miscellaneous tenures which cannot properly be grouped under either of these heads.

I. *The Survey Tenure.*—The Survey tenure is that upon which the ordinary government land is held. It may be subdivided into two classes, *viz.*, the Old or Unrestricted, and the New or Restricted Tenure. Under the old tenure the occupant holds the land with full rights of disposal either by sale, mortgage, lease or other form of transfer subject only to the payment of the government assessment. He has also the right to all trees on the land with certain exceptions: he has also the right to make any improvements in his holding secure in the belief that no extra assessment will ever be charged for the same: at his death the land descends to his heirs. The only obligations imposed on him are those of paying the assessment, keeping up his boundary marks, providing flagholders and chainmen, if necessary, for survey work and giving notice of changes for the purposes of the Record-of-Rights. If at any time he wishes to do so, he can resign his land and so suit the extent of his possessions to his resources.

Under the New Tenure the occupant has the same privileges except that freedom of transfer whether by sale, mortgage or lease is forbidden except by the permission of the Collector. This form of the Survey tenure was introduced in 1901 by an amendment to the Land Revenue Code. Its main object was to secure the land of the more improvident classes of cultivators from falling into the hands of the *saukár*, which would inevitably have happened had the old tenure been extended to lands granted them.

II. *Inam Tenures.*—The word 'Inam' means 'gift' or 'grant'; and land held on an Inam tenure is that in respect of which there has been an alienation of part or all of its rights by government on behalf of one or more individuals.

An enquiry into the validity of titles to such alienated holdings was tentatively commenced in 1843 in one or two collectorates of the Southern Mahratha country, and, in consequence of the discovery of unauthorized and fraudulent alienations it was developed in 1851 into an organized investigation, which under the title of the Inam Commission or Alienation Department extended to the whole of the Presidency. The Commission at first instituted detailed enquires into the different titles submitted to it, but after a time this procedure was found inconveniently slow, and two Acts were passed (Act 2 of 1863 for the Deccan, Khandesh and Southern Mahratha country, and Act 7 of 1863 for Gujarat and the Konkan) giving persons who claimed exemption from the payment of full government revenue the option of avoiding scrutiny of their title by the payment of quit-rent. This quickened operations and by 1873 the bulk of the work was finished.

For all practical purposes the tenures on which alienated holdings are now continued may be reduced to the following four principal clauses:—

(1) Political, (2) Service, (3) Religious, (4) Personal.

(1) *Political.*—Under the head of 'political tenure' are included political pensions and what are known as *jaghirs* and *saranjams.* Grants of this description are to be found almost exclusively in the collectorates of the Southern Division and in the Nasik and Khandesh Districts of the Central Division. *Jaghir and saranjam,* though the former is a term of Mahomedan and the latter of Mahratha origin, are understood to have similar characteristics, having been originally grants by the state for the performance of civil or military duties, or for the maintenance of the personal dignity of nobles and high officials. Under the British government, however, no such distinctions are preserved; and the *jaghirs* and *saranjams* now in existence have, with some exceptions, where service is commuted into money payments, no condition of service attached to them, but are continued hereditarily, or for one or more generations on political considerations alone.

(2) *Service Tenure.*—The assignments of land or of money, held on what is known as 'service tenures,' are grants which impose duties on the holders. Such grants were originally made with a view to ensure the performance of certain services in each district and for each village. As no change has been introduced in the constitution of village communities, village service is still rendered in return for the grant of land or of money. But by the introduction of the revenue survey and the organization of a stipendiary police, the former system of district service became obsolete, and the duties of the holders of district service assignments ceased. An arrangement has

accordingly been introduced under which the holders of such assignments become, on repaying a portion of their emoluments, free from all liability to serve.

(3) *Religious Tenure.*—Holdings granted by the former native governments for the support of Hindu and Mahomedan religious or charitable institutions, such as temples, mosques, &c., and continued under the British government, come under the head 'religious tenure.' Such holdings are tenable in perpetuity, or so long as the institutions for the maintenance of which they were originally granted or are now held may be in existence. They are entered in the public accounts under the head of *devasthan.*

(4) *Personal Tenure.*—The head of 'personal tenure' comprises that vast body of holdings which, though alienated by the former governments under various denominations, have been continued without any distinguishing peculiarity simply as personal *inams* or unconditional grants enjoyed by individuals. Under the operation of the Summary Settlement Acts (Bombay Acts 2 and 7 of 1863) and other subsidiary settlements, personal *inams* are for the most part continuable in perpetuity, and are transferable without any restriction whatsoever. Those, however, which do not come under the summary settlement mentioned above, do not carry with them the right of adoption.

III. *Miscellaneous Tenures.*—The remaining tenures of the Presidency are the following:—

(*a*) GUJARAT.

(*i*) The Talukdari Tenure.

The Talukdari Tenure is one of the most important in Gujarat. It prevails in the districts of Ahmedabad, Kaira Broach and Panch Mahals, the greater number of estates held under this tenure being situated in the Western talukas of Ahmedabad adjoining Kathiawar, *viz.*, Dhandhuka, Dholka, Gogha and Viramgam.

The leading characteristic of Talukdari tenure is that a Talukdari estate is held neither in gift from the Crown (i.e., 'alienated'), nor in occupancy (i.e., 'unalienated') but with full proprietary rights antedating the advent of British rule and including ownership of mines, minerals and trees.

All Talukdari estates are held subject to the payment of *jama* (land revenue) to government which may either be *udhad* (fixed in perpetuity), or fluctuating. The estates in Kaira and Broach are mostly held on *udhad jama* or quit-rent fixed under the Summary Settlement Act, while those in Ahmedabad pay *jama* which is liable to revision on expiry of a term of settlement not exceeding 30 years.

Origin of Tulukdars.—The Talukdars of Gujarat are historically identical with the ruling families of Kathiawar and other agencies, and their loss of political power is generally ascribed to the geographical accident of their estates being situated in the *rasti* (settled) portion of the province which was brought under the direct rule of the Paramount Power, while their kinsmen in the *mulkgiri* (unsettled) portion continued to be treated as tributaries. The Talukdars comprise men of varying position, ranging from jurisdictional chiefs holding talukdari villages in British districts and the holders of recognised chieftainships such as sanand, gamph, etc., to the holders of a few acres in a co-parcenary estate who are fast being converted into yeomen cultivators.

Alienations.—Talukdari estates contain large areas of of land given to cadets, widows of the family and other relatives for maintenance, and to village servants and others either in reward for past services or as remuneration for services still being performed. Service lands falling within the last category are resumable at will, and in other cases the Talukdar has a right of reversion on the failure of male heirs. These inferior holders generally contribute little to the state though in some cases a small quit-rent is chargeable.

Under the Talukdari Act a talukdar is forbidden to encumber his estate beyond his lifetime without the sanction of the talukdari settlement officer and cannot alienate the same without the sanction of government. Ordinarily government does not interfere with the management of estates, but under certain conditions they can be taken under the management of the special talukdari settlement officer.

(*ii*) *The Vanta Tenure.*—The word 'Vanta' means "divided" and the origin of the tenure is supposed to be the action of the Mahomedan invaders of Gujarat who deprived the original chiefs of all land held by them except one-fourth, which was called 'Vanta.' Some of these 'Vanta' lands are held free, but most pay a quit-rent to government.

(*iii*) *The Mehwasi Tenure.*—The Mehwasidars are the descendants of Mehwasi Koli or Rajput chiefs. Certain villages were granted them, really by way of blackmail, on the condition of their keeping open certain woods, or refraining from plundering certain districts and so on. These villages are now held subject to the payment of a quit-rent to government.

In the Kalol taluka of the Panch mahals district certain villages are held on a similar tenure by a class of headmen called 'Mehwasi Patels.'

(*iv*) *The Maleki Tenure.*—The Maleks are the descendants of certain Mussalman families known as 'malikjadas' who were granted lands by Mahammad Begari, the Sultan of Ahmedabad, some four centuries ago for gallantry at the capture of Pavagad, a celebrated hill-fortress in the Panch Mahals district. They were originally granted rent free, but a tribute was eventually imposed at the time of the Mahratta dominion. Under the present settlement the village revenues are shared between government and the Maleks, the shares of the latter ranging from 7 to 9 annas.

(*v*) *The Narvadari and Bhagdari Tenures.*—Villages held on these tenures which are of the same class exist mainly in the districts of Kaira and Broach. The peculiarity of the tenure is that the villages are held by bodies of joint proprietors called 'narvadars' or 'bhagdars. Most of the village land is divided into main shares called 'muksh bhags' and these again into minor shares or 'peta bhags' which have resulted from the sub-division of the 'muksh bhags' on inheritance. There is also sometimes an area called 'majmun' which is common either to the whole village or to certain of the individual shares.

All these villages have been surveyed and settled according to the Bombay system and the proprietors are liable to pay the full government assessment on the village lands. This payment is made not according to the area actually held by any particular share, but on the basis of the old traditional sub-division of the assessment called the 'phalaoni,' the share of each 'bhag' being entitled the 'phala.'

Persons cultivating the village lands are the tenants of the Bhagdars and are of two kinds, *viz.* tenants-at-will and customary tenants, who have a permanent tenure so long as they pay the assessment.

(*b*) The Konkan.

(*i*) *The Khoti Tenure.*—The true Khoti tenure is that found in the Kolaba and Ratnagiri collectorates. Villages held on this tenure are in the possession of individuals called 'khots' who are limited proprietors. In origin they were probably farmers who were granted leases for the improvement of the country, but gained certain proprietary rights by prescription. They hold their villages subject to the payment of the government assessment, in default of which the village may be attached.

The lands are cultivated by their tenants of whom those called 'dharekaris' pay the survey assessment only, while the others pay varying amounts in addition to the survey assessment.

(*ii*) *The Shilotri Tenure.*—'Shilotri' lands are those which have been reclaimed from the sea and the permanence of which depends upon the embankments being kept up. The descendants of those who carried out the reclamation work hold these lands upon condition either of keeping up the embankments themselves or else having a levy made which is appropriated to the work.

(*c*) General.

The Sharakali Tenure.—All over the Presidency there are a number of villages held on this tenure, the main feature of which is that the village revenues are shared between government and the holder in a fixed proportion ranging from 10 to 6 annas as the share of the latter.

PUNJAB

Character of Land Tenures and System of Survey and Settlements.

Based on the Administration Report of the Punjab, 1911-12.

Proprietorships.—Taking the British districts of the province as a whole it may be estimated that about one-sixth of the area is the property of government, the remaining five-sixths belonging to private owners. A large part of the area belonging to government is so situated that it cannot be brought under cultivation without the aid of extensive works of irrigation. The Lower Chenab Canal irrigates some 1,900,000 acres of what was formerly government waste land and the Lower Jhelum Canal, an additional 360,000 acres. The Lower Bari Doab Canal now approaching completion will command an additional area of government waste. Large areas in the hills and elsewhere, which are unsuited for cultivation, are preserved as forest or grazing lands, and others in addition to the colony lands are held under lease from government for purposes of cultivation. The proportion of cultivated land owned by government to that owned by private individuals is at present about one to twelve.

Land Revenue.—All land is held subject to the payment of land revenue to the State, or to grantees holding from the State, unless such liability has been redeemed or compounded for. In some cases the assignments are of the nature of the release of the revenue of lands belonging to the assignees but have no necessary connection with proprietary right; and in the majority of instances the grantees are merely entitled to receive the revenue payable to government, the amount of which is limited in the same way as if it were paid direct to government.

Land Alienation Act.—The fatal facility with which the agricultural tribes of the Punjab had got into the clutches of money-lenders, resulting in the course of time in the reduction in their status from proprietors to tenants, had long been marked, and remedies discussed for arresting this tendency. The outcome of years of discussion was Act 13 of 1900, which limits the free transfer of landed property by persons who are declared to be members of agricultural tribes to members of the same tribe, or of a tribe in the same group. Transfers of land by such people to others not so specified require the consent of the Deputy Cammissioner, for whose guidance explicit rules have been laid down. The Act also places restrictions on mortgages to non-agriculturists. The original Act permitted free transfers to "agriculturists," (an "agriculturist" meaning a person holding agricultural land either in his own name or that of an ancestor in the male line as an owner or hereditary tenant from the time of the first regular settlement of the district in which the land is situate, or from such other date as government may determine). This power was taken away by an Amending Act in 1907. The Act has been sympathetically administered, and has so far fulfilled the hopes with which it was framed. Opposed, of course, by the classes against whose acquisitive activities it was directed, it has been acquiesced in both because of its popularity with the preponderant agricultural population whom it protects from the effects of their ignorance and folly, and also because of the opening of new spheres of investment in the development of which it has been the care of government to assist. Fears that agricultural credit would be destroyed have proved groundless, and the price of land now stands far higher than even before the passing of the Act.

Rights of pre-emption.—The great mass of the landed property in the Punjab is held by small proprietors, who cultivate their own land in whole or in part. The chief characteristic of the tenure generally is that these proprietors are associated together in village communities, having to a greater or less extent joint interests, and, under our system of cash payments limited so as to secure a certain profit to the proprietors, jointly responsible for the payment of the revenue assessed upon the village lands. It is an incident of the tenure, that if any of the proprietors wishes to sell his rights, or is obliged to part with them in order to satisfy demands upon him, the other members of the same community have a preferential right to purchase them at the same price as could be obtained from outsiders.

Punjab Pre-emption Act.—The recasting of the law of pre-emption was one of the corollaries to the passing of the Punjab Alienation of Land Act. The new law came into force as Punjab Act 2 of 1905, its chief aim being to prevent a non-agriculturist when he has once gained a footing in a village community from buying up other shares in the village as they come into the market, and so expropriating the true agriculturist and breaking up the village community. The pre-emption law is admittedly unsatisfactory and gives rise to abuses, particularly in the form of bogus threats by persons with rights of pre-emption to enforce these rights when a sale of land is in question. A considerable body of opinion is now in existence especially among judicial officers that the time has come to sweep away the whole system as an archaic survival no longer in keeping with modern conditions.

Zamindari Tenures.—In some cases (technically known as zamindari tenures) all the proprietors have an undivided interest in all the land belonging to the proprietary community; in other words, all the land is in common, and what the proprietors themselves cultivate is held by them as tenants of the community. Their rights are regulated by their shares in the estates, both as regards the extent of the holdings they are entitled to cultivate, and as regards the distribution of profits; and, if the profits from land held by non-proprietary cultivators are not sufficient to pay the revenue and other charges, the balance would ordinarily be collected from the proprietors according to the same shares.

Separate holdings.—It is, however, much more common for the proprietors to have their own separate holdings in the estate, and this separation may extend so far that there is no land susceptible of separate appropriation which is not the separate property of an individual or family. In an extreme case like this the right of pre-emption and the joint responsibility for the revenue, should any of the individual proprietors fail to meet the demand upon him, are almost the only ties which bind the community together. The separation, however, generally does not go so far. Often all the cultivated land is held in separate ownership, while the pasture, village site, roads, ponds or tanks, &c., remain in common. In other cases land cultivated by tenants is the common property of the community, and it frequently happens that the village contains several well-known sub-divisions, each with its own separate land, the whole of which may be held in common by the proprietors of the sub-division, or the whole may be held in severalty, or part in separate ownership and part in common.

Pattidari and Bhaiyachara Tenures.—In those communities (technically known as *bhaiyachara* and *pattidari*) with partial or entire separation of proprietary title, the measure of the rights and liabilities of the proprietors varies very much. It sometimes depends solely upon original acquisition and the operation of the laws of inheritance; in other cases definite shares in the land of a village or sub-division different from those which would result from the law of inheritance have been established by custom; in other cases reference is made not to shares in the land, but to shares in a well, or other source of irrigation; and in the majority of cases in the east and south-east of the Punjab no specified shares are any longer acknowledged, but the area in the separate possession of each proprietor is the sole measure of his interest. Where the rights and liabilities are determined according to certain known shares, the tenure is known as *pattidari;* where possession is the measure of each man's right and liability, it is called *bhaiyachara.* It is sometimes the case, however, that while the separate holdings do not correspond with any recognized shares, such shares will be regarded in dividing the profits of common land, or in the partition of such land and wells are generally held according to shares, even where the title to the land depends exclusively on undisturbed possession.

Village Communities.—Throughout a great part of the province the organization of the proprietors of land into village communities has existed from time immemorial, and is the work of the people themselves, and not the result of measures adopted either by our own, or by previous, governments. Indeed, these communities have sometimes been strong enough to resist the payment of revenue to the government of the day, and before our rule nothing was more common than for them to decide their disputes by petty wars against each other, instead of having recourse to any superior authority to settle them. But in some localities the present communities have been constituted from motives of convenience in the application of our system of settlement. Thus in the Simla hills, and in the more mountainous portions of the Kangra district, the present village communities consist of numerous small hamlets, each with its own group of fields and separate lands, and which had no bond of union until they were united for administrative purposes at the time of the land revenue settlement. In the south-western districts, again, while regular village communities were frequently found in the fertile lands fringing the rivers, all trace of these disappeared where the cultivation was dependent on scattered wells beyond the immediate influence of the river. Here the well was the true unit of property ; but where the proprietors of several wells lived together for mutual protection, or their wells were sufficiently near to be conveniently included within one village boundary, the opportunity was taken to group them into village communities. These arrangements were made possible by the circumstance that the village community system admits of any amount of separation of the property of the individual proprietors, and by care being taken that in the internal distribution of the revenue demand it should be duly adjusted with reference to the resources of the separate holdings. They also in general involved the making over in joint ownership to the proprietors of the separate holdings of waste land situate within the new boundary, in which no private property had previously existed.

Quit-rent payments.—In some cases the village communities, while holding and managing the land as proprietors (*adna malik*), are bound to pay quit-rent to the superior proprietors (*ala malik*), under whom they hold. The settlement is now required to be made in such circumstances with the communities in actual possession of the land, who pay the land revenue to government and the quit-rent to the superior proprietor ; but in special cases the Financial Commissioners may order the settlement to be made with the superior proprietor. The amount which the superior proprietor is entitled to collect is determined at settlement as well as the amount of the land revenue demand.

Limited Proprietors.—There are sometimes also proprietors holding lands within the estates of village communities, but who are not members of the communities, and are not entitled to share in the common profit, nor liable for anything more than the revenue of their own lands, the village charges ordinarily paid by proprietors, and the quit-rent, if any, payable to the proprietary body of the village. The most common examples of this class are the holders of plots at present or formerly revenue-free, in which the assignees were allowed to get proprietary possession in consequence of having planted gardens, or made other improvements, or because they had other claims to consideration on the part of the village community. In the Rawalpindi division also it was thought proper to record old-established tenants, who had never paid anything for the land they held, but their proportion of the land revenue and village expenses, and had long paid direct to the collectors of the revenue, but were not descended from the original proprietary body, as owners of their own holdings, while not participating in the common rights and liabilities of the proprietary community. Except in the Jhelum and Rawalpindi districts, where a small quit-rent was in some cases imposed, these inferior proprietors, called *malik kabza*, were not required to pay anything in excess of their proportion of the government revenue and other village charges. In *Gujrat*, at the time of the first regular settlement, this class held no less than 10 per cent. of the total cultivated area, and in Rawalpindi it paid 9 per cent. of the revenue. In Rawalpindi the persons recorded as proprietors of their own holdings only were in some cases the representatives of the original proprietary body, jagirdars having established proprietary rights over what were formerly the common lands of the village.

Settlements.—With the exception of a few estates of which the revenue has been redeemed by the proprietors under a policy long since abandoned, the village assessments are revised from time to time, the term of settlement being usually thirty years in the case of fully developed districts and twenty years where conditions are less advanced. Re-assessment has, hitherto, usually been by a special revision of the records, though the processes are quite distinct; and a general revision could not until recently be undertaken without the sanction of the Government of India. The rule laying down the standard of assessment is as follows:—"The assessment of an estate will be fixed according to circumstances, but must not exceed half the value of the net assets," a phrase which is defined as meaning "the average surplus which the estate may yield after deduction of the expenses of cultivation, including profits of stock and wages of labour." When the rents are fair competition rents, 50 per cent. of the rental is considered to be the measure of the half assets share of rented land and the rates ascertained from these rents for all classes of soil are applied to the whole cultivation, whether by tenants or by the owners. The ascertainment of the rental is a comparatively easy matter with our present records where cash rents prevail, but considerable difficulty is encountered in converting produce rents into a cash rate. The area of each crop is of course known, but estimates have to be made of the outturns of each crop, the actual share received by the landlord and the prices obtained by him for his produce; all of which, owing to the uncertainty involved, are probably usually under-estimated. In practice, it is recognized that there are many reasons which may justify a Settlement Officer in assessing below the maximum standard, but he is required to state as accurately as possible what the half net assets are, and to give good reasons for any proposal to fix the government demand much below that standard. No particular fraction of the *gross produce* is prescribed as the limit of the land revenue demand, the only limit being that just mentioned, namely, half the value of the net assets. The actual assessment nowhere exceeds one-fifth of the gross produce. It is more often equal to one-seventh, one-eighth, or even a smaller fraction. There is a marked tendency in the recent assessment policy of the Punjab to assess irrigation from wells with greater leniency than before, in consideration of the expenditure of capital and labour in constructing and working the well, and very liberal rules are now in force postponing the full assessment on new wells for a term of years and remitting part of the demand when the well falls in. Whether for cash or produce rent areas the present practice is for the Settlement Officer to submit his assessment proposals in a report dealing usually with a tahsil, through the *Commissioner to the Financial Commissioners* who pass the necessary orders which, after they have been submitted to Government for confirmation, are communicated to the Settlement Officer for compliance.

Forms of assessment.—The usual form of demand is an assessment fixed for a term of years and realisable (subject to suspensions and remissions) in good and bad years alike; but systems of fluctuating assessments, under which the harvest demand is ascertained by the application of sanctioned rates to the harvest area, have long been a feature of Punjab land revenue administration. Much progress has been made in recent years in the simplification and improvement of the rules under which the assessments are carried out, and since the last revision of settlement in Multan, increasingly large areas are assessed in this way, especially in the west of the province. Within the last ten years the fixed Government demand has dropped from Rs. 222 lakhs to Rs. 214 lakhs, while the fluctuating demand has in the same period risen from Rs. 31 lakhs to Rs. 71 lakhs. On these figures the percentage of the total demand assessed on the fluctuating principle has more than doubled in ten years and now amounts to one quarter of the whole. It has, however, to be remembered that it is extremely difficult, in present circumstances of development, to obtain an idea of the normal fluctuating demand, and again that, though the fluctuating demand is generally collected in full, much of the fixed demand is suspended and eventually remitted.

THE UNITED PROVINCES.

Based on the Administration Report of the United Provinces, 1911-1912.

The Land Revenue system.—The provinces are essentially agricultural: at the last census some 72 per cent. of the total population was found to depend on agriculture for its chief source of income. It is not surprising therefore to find that the history of British administration is closely bound up with the history of its land revenue system. This ultimately rests on the principle, clearly enunciated in Regulation 31 of 1803, that "by the ancient law of the country the ruling power is entitled to a certain proportion of the annual produce of every bigha of land." Under ALA-UD-DIN KHILIJI (A.D. 1316) the land revenue was 50 per cent. of the produce: under GHIYAS-UD-DIN TUGHLAK, five or six years later, it was 10 per cent. A revenue based on the produce was a system only workable in a primitive society where there could be direct communication between ruler and ruled. It is clear that such communication was not possible for very long, or for very long at a time. In the constant round of wars and invasions, chiefs were continually setting themselves up as petty rulers who took the payments of the cultivators and themselves paid tribute to the KING. The settlement of invaders on the land (and the history of castes is full of stories of such settlements) the grants of lands to the kinsmen or followers of such chiefs, the land-grabbing of officials and speculators, all operated to interpose several interests between that of the King and that of the cultivator. One of the first problems of British rule was to straighten out the tangle of consequent rights and their corresponding duties.

Tenures before British rule.—Proprietary rights in land occasionally existed before British rule, but were not strictly defined. In most places the system was *zamindari*, where the owner or co-owners were jointly responsible for the payment of the land revenue of the whole village: but in Bundelkhand and Kumaun it was *ryotwari*, where each several cultivator was responsible for the land revenue due on his own land. This is a distinction which, though no longer recognized, has left its mark on the modern land revenue system, and joint responsibility is still enforced with difficulty in some parts of the province. In some districts double rights existed, mostly in estates known as *taluqdari*, where the inferior proprietors were known as *zamindars, biswadars, britias*, &c. Some of the taluqdars were representatives of those old princes who had held authority over large areas: others were officials who had acquired similar authority, or grantees and contractors. These had interposed themselves between the lesser proprietors and the supreme authority, and, in the disorders of the 18th century, had swallowed up the property of the former either by forcibly dispossessing them, or by receiving a voluntary submission. On the other hand, the taluqdars had been in the habit of granting subordinate rights in parts of their hereditary domains, of which the most common was *birt* or "cession." These grants were made for money payment, or in return for services of various kinds. There were, and are, also other similar subordinate rights extending only to specific plots instead of to a whole village.

Growth of the present Land Revenue system.—In 1788 MR. JONATHAN DUNCAN was authorized to amend the system of revenue management in the Benares division, which was oppressive and caused much distress; the revenue was simply levied at the highest sum which anybody would offer. He obtained valuations of the produce of parganas and fixed standard rates for different classes of soil.

The Permanent Settlement of Benares.—His summary settlement was revised carefully with a view to making the demand permanent and after a few corrections was declared unalterable by Regulation 1 of 1795.

Ceded and Conquered districts.—It was at first desired to introduce a similar permanent settlement in what is now the province of Agra. There were to be two settlements for 3 years each, and a third for 4 years, after which the demand was to be fixed in perpetuity. But the Court of Directors refused to sanction a permanent settlement, and short term assessments continued. The system was far from satisfactory. There were no data available on which to base the estimates, save the statements of the kanungos and the accounts of the patwaris, both unreliable, and checked only by information given by the zamindar's enemies. The assessments were very uneven: and since at first (till 1806) the tashildars were paid by a percentage on collections, they were interested in high revenues and full collections. The natural result was corruption of all kinds; and in 1807 a special commission was appointed to supervise the settlements, which grew into the western Board of Revenue. Matters improved with each successive settlement, but the Collectors could deal only with persons actually in possession, and the courts were not numerous enough, nor able, to cope with claims to recover possession. The result of this was the special commission appointed by Regulation 1 of 1821 to consider such claims, which sat till 1829 when its powers were transferred to the Commissioners of Revenue and Circuit. In 1835 the powers were withdrawn and transferred to the ordinary courts.

Mr. Mackenzie's Memorandum of 1819 and Regulation 7 of 1822.—In 1819 Mr. Holt Mackenzie in a remarkable memorandum which covered the whole ground once more urged the need of a permanent settlement. Though the Directors refused again to commit themselves to this, they approved of his suggestion for a complete inquiry and the result was Regulation 7 of 1822. This laid down new and improved methods of assessment, including a complete record of rights of all kinds, a full account of the rates of cash rents, and the method of division of produce where grain rents existed, a survey, and the maintenance of village records and the establishment of revenue courts. The assessment was to be such as to leave the zamindars a profit of 20 per cent. on their revenue. Though the Regulation marks the first advance towards a systematic assessment on the rental assets of each village, it involved most elaborate and minute inquiries and in 1830 the Board went so far as to describe the system as unworkable. At last matters came to a head in 1832-33. The impossible method of determining the assets on estimates of the produce of each field was denounced by MR. BIRD: a few officers had already realized that the simplest way to ascertain the assets was to obtain a correct rent roll. At last the matter was focussed by LORD WILLIAM BENTINCK's minute of the 26th September 1832.

Regulation 9 of 1833.—In this minute he laid down seven principles of action. A professional survey was to take the place of the *amin* establishment; the assessment was to be fixed on a general knowledge of the aggregate cultivated area of an estate and its special advantages; the apportionment in detail of the assessment was to be left to the landlords: the settlement officer's judicial powers were to be restricted; existing institutions and systems of village management were not to be interfered with: all existing rights and privileges were to be secured; and the patwari establishment was to be put on an efficient footing. These principles were accepted by Regulation 9 of 1833 which laid down the new procedure. Village maps, a field book, a rent roll, and statements of the revenue demand, receipts and balances were drawn up, and the revenue demand was fixed on a consideration of these papers. Incidentally, the Regulation created the appointment of deputy collectors.

First Regular Settlement.—On these lines the first regular settlement was completed by MESSRS. BIRD and THOMASON between the years 1833 and 1849 and was confirmed for 30 years. Its results may be summarized as follows:—

(1) Settlement was made wherever possible with village proprietors; and the ryotwari system of Bundelkhand was replaced by a zamindari system with joint responsibility. In the eastern districts the subordinate proprietors or *birtias* were given full proprietary rights. The taluqdar generally disappeared save in rare cases where the village proprietors desired the connection to continue, in which case their payments to him where fixed; elsewhere the taluqdar received a rent charge or malikana, originally fixed at 18 per cent. on the assets. The taluqdari system is now rare in Agra.

(2) Hereditary tenants, and tenants who had resided and cultivated in the same village for 12 years, were given rights of occupancy when they claimed them, or even when they did not claim them, if the local officer thought they might have done so.

(3) The assessments were on the whole moderate; though they amounted on an average to 66 per cent. of the rental assets.

Saharanpur Settlement.—In 1855 the proportion of the assets to be taken as revenue was fixed at 50 instead of 66 per cent., and this standard has been retained to the present day, though it is unusual now to take a full half of the assets as revenue. The assets to be taken into account were at the same time defined to be the ***net average assets*** subject to certain corrections.

Second regular Settlement in Agra.—In the second regular settlement there were various improvements. As stated above, the assessment had been based upon the average rental assets, but the patwaris' papers were still far from reliable and the assets were calculated on the rates of rent actually found to be paid in the locality. The soils were now classified, at first field by field, but afterwards (1868) by a system of demarcating blocks of soils, and standard rates of rent were fixed for each class. The assessment was based upon this estimated rental, which might be higher than the amount actually paid, but represented the sum which could be realized.

Third regular Settlement.—In 1884-86 revised rules were issued providing for more careful preparation and check of the patwari's record so as to form a reliable basis of assessment. The change lay in the fact that whilst the circle rent rate, ascertained by inquiry and selection, had formerly been the basis of assessment, the actual rent-roll now became that basis and the circle rent rate was used as a check. At the same time all consideration of prospective increase in value was definitely excluded from the assets, and concessions were made to private individuals for improvements made by them. The method of survey and revision of records was materially cheapened, and the principle that existing settlements should be continued where no substantial enhancement was likely to occur was accepted. The settlement of a district now takes three years instead of from six to ten years.

First Summary Settlement of Oudh.—When Oudh was annexed in 1856 Lord Dalhousie decided to introduce the system of settlement with the village proprietors. The principle was carried out with a lack of consideration for the great taluqdari families of the province which was probably never intended, and the taluqdars were ousted from the greater parts of their estates, sometimes even from their own hereditary villages. After the mutiny however, LORD CANNING reverted to a taluqdari settlement. He had, he wrote, lost faith in the stability of the village system even in the older provinces, for many proprietors had acknowledged the suzerainty of the former taluqdars as soon as British rule was subverted ; it was obvious that the taluqdari system was "the ancient, indigenous and cherished system of the country :" and if this was so in Agra it would be much more so in Oudh, where village occupancy independent of taluqdars was unknown.

Second Summary Settlement of Oudh.—The result was the second summary settlement of Oudh in 1858, by which the taluqdars were given full proprietary rights in all the villages which they held at annexation and the gift was confirmed by *sanad.*

Recognition of inferior rights in taluqas.—It was originally provided that the rights of the under-proprietors or "parties holding an intermediate interest in the land between the taluqdar and the ryot," were to be maintained as they existed in 1855. The taluqdars moreover agreed to waive their *sanads* as regards lands mortgaged to them within 12 years before annexation with no fixed term for redemption, and also all those in which a term had been fixed which had not expired before annexation. Apart from such lands the sanads were final and village proprietors could only claim under-proprietary rights.

At a later date (1860), however, the question of subordinate rights in Oudh again came up ; and after much discussion it was held to be proved that there was no such thing as tenant right in Oudh before annexation ; the gift of under-proprietary rights was limited to those who had enjoyed proprietary rights within twelve years of annexation, whilst occupancy rights were conferred on all tenants who had been in proprietary possession within 30 years of annexation. These under-proprietary rights range from sub-settlements of whole villages to rights in specific plots.

Finally, by Act 1 of 1869 the privileges of the taluqdars, the power of making a will, and the special rules for intestate succession (which amounted to this, that the condition of primogeniture was recognized in such cases if the taluqdar himself desired that it should be so), were confirmed.

The question of a Permanent Settlement :—It has already been stated that a permanent settlement was introduced into the province of Benares, the first part of the present province of Agra to come under British rule. A similar settlement was proposed for the "ceded and conquered districts" which became British territory a few years later; but the Directors of the East India Company would not allow it and the proposal was revived in 1819 and again negatived. In 1860, the question was once more revived and was discussed during several years. By that time, however, the probable inequalities arising from the different stages of development in different tracts were realised and for this reason, but largely on financial grounds, the question was finally dropped in 1874. A kindred proposal was, however, started in 1882. The scheme then put forward contemplated an increase of revenue only in case of an increase in production due to improvements made at government expense. This proposal was ultimately considered to be impracticable and it, too, was dropped in 1885.

Present methods of assessment.—The first object of the settlement officer employed to revise an assessment of land revenue is to ascertain the assets of which the prescribed percentage is to be taken. For this purpose he examines the rental as recorded in the village papers and tests it in order to judge whether it is fair or excessive or inadequate, and to ascertain whether it is correctly recorded or part of it is concealed in order to defraud the government. To carry out this test he divides the tract under assessment into circles containing villages of similar character and marks off on the map of each village the different classes of soil. For each class of soil in each circle he ascertains the fair rate of rent usually paid by the tenants, and by the rates so found he tests the rent roll of each village. If, considering the quality of the village as compared with the average, the recorded rental is approximately the same as the valuation by his rates, the settlement officer usually accepts it as genuine and adequate. If, again making allowances for the quality of the village, the settlement officer finds the rental as recorded to be too high to be regularly collected, he will reject a suitable portion of it for the purposes of assessment and take the remainder only into account in calculating the assets. If, on the other hand, the rental appears too low and it can be immediately enhanced (as in the case of occupancy tenants in Agra) he will substitute an enhanced rental, and will, on the application of the proprietor, fix the rents of occupancy tenants at a higher rate for the future. There are, however, some lands which are not rented, such as the proprietor's home farm (*sir or khudkasht*) and land given to village servants or to dependants in lieu of wages or maintenance. Such land has to be valued, and it is usually valued at the soil rates of the circle, raised or lowered according to the quality of the particular village. The valuation of such unrented lands is added to the rental of the tenants, adjusted as above described, and the gross assets of the village are thus found. From this total are deducted certain allowances made as a concession to proprietors on account of their own cultivation, or for improvements (such as the sinking of wells) carried out at the proprietor's expense, and the result is the *net assets* on which the assessment of the revenue is based. As already mentioned, the standard of the revenue is half the net assets, but the full half is now seldom taken unless the enhancement is very small or for other exceptional reasons."

Term of settlement.—The term of settlement is now 30 years except in some precarious or deteriorated tracts, where five years' settlements are given. In the case of landowners, who conceal their true rentals (the number is small) short-term settlements are also usually given. Special rules provide for the settlement of villages which are exposed to diluvion. Special short-term settlements are also in force in Bundelkhand, where owing to the precarious nature of the outlying cultivation due to a constant liability to drought or the spread of *kans* grass, the cultivated area is classed as *established* and *nautor* (*i.e.*, land nearly broken up), the latter being valued for assessment purposes at a customary low rate. Variations of over 10 per cent. in the area of established cultivation result in a revision of the assessment and all villages come under scrutiny according to a roster once in 5 years. If, however, any village shows a decrease of 15 per cent. the landholder may apply for a revision within the quinquennial period.

Character of Land Tenures.

Proprietary right in theory and practice.—Proprietary right now corresponds with the obligation to pay the land revenue, where the land revenue has not been remitted assigned or redeemed.* Legally, in Agra and the non-taluqdari estates in Oudh, the right grows up out of this obligation ; in taluqdari estates in Oudh the obligation legally follows the right. In practice the right and the obligation have become inseparable in the former case.

* Where the land revenue has been remitted, assigned or redeemed, the proprietary right resides in the person or persons, who, but for such remission, assignation or redemption would have been liable to pay the land revenue, and who, in fact, pay the local rates.

Historically, the distinction has been important only in the treatment of inferior proprietary interests. In Agra there can legally be and are, in non-taluqdari estates in Oudh there might legally be, but are not. two proprietary interests in the same land. In taluqdari estates in Oudh there can legally be only one proprietary interest.

In practice however there is only one proprietary right in both provinces. In Agra, where the settlement has been made with the holders of the inferior interest, the holder of the superior interest is merely an assignee or stipendiary ; where, on the other hand, the settlement has been made with the holder of the superior interest, the holders of the inferior interest are inferior proprietors. In Oudh all recognized inferior proprietary interests are under-proprietary.

It is important to remember that the word *taluqdar* has had a different meaning and effect in the two provinces. In Agra, where it is no longer used, it meant a person who was originally the holder of the superior of two proprietary interests, and is now an assignee or actual proprietor : in Oudh it means an opulent and privileged land-owner, whose rights are secured by a *sanad* and confirmed by law.

Tenures.—The settlement of the United Provinces is called *zamindari* in contradistinction to *ryotwari*. In that sense all proprietors, including taluqdars in Oudh, are zamindars or persons who may receive rent from cultivators and must pay land revenue to government. Apart from the taluqdari estates in Oudh, which are a thing *per se*, the proprietary tenures are similar in the two provinces, *viz.* :—

(i) *Single zamindari.*—Where there is one proprietor ;

(ii) *Joint zamindari.*—Where there are more than one proprietor who hold the land in common ;

(iii) *Pattidari.*—Where there are more than one proprietor who hold the land separately, and whose interests are recorded by fractional shares ;

(iv) *Bhaiyachara.*—Where there are more proprietors than one who hold the land separately, and whose interests are recorded by the areas actually in the possession of each ;

(v) *Imperfect pattidari or bhaiyachara.*—Where there are more than one proprietor who hold part of the land in common, and part separately on either tenure.

In origin the *pattidari* tenure is disintegrated *joint zamindari.* In origin the *bhaiyachara* tenure is either disintegrated *joint zamindari* where the fractional shares have been lost sight of, or ryotwari articulated by joint responsibility.

Mahals and Joint Responsibility.—The unit of revenue management is the mahal, or estate, which may be one village or several villages, or part of one village, or parts of several villages. All the proprietors of a mahal (*i.e.* where the tenure is not single zemindari) are jointly and severally responsible for the land revenue fixed on the mahal. Joint responsibility is the distinguishing feature of the *zamindari* form of settlement.

Originally the land revenue was paid where there were more than one proprietor, through representatives or *lambardars* elected by the proprietors concerned subject to the approval of the collector. The tendency to fission which is the unavoidable result of peace and good government is acting as a solvent on the principle of joint responsibility, and the *lambardari* system is breaking down. The "little republics" of Sir C. Metcalfe's picture if they ever existed have long since disappeared. In parts of the province the continued subdivision of proprietary holding is already realizing the fear of Mr. Holt Mackenzie that "we may speedily have a system of management even more detailed than the ryotwari." Where the principle of joint responsibility has already broken down, tbe *zamindari* is in fact degenerating into the ryotwari form of settlement. The process of *morcellement*, however, tends to correct itself, as wealthier co-sharers buy up the shares of their poorer brethren and the Land Revenue Act of 1901 attempts to strengthen the *lambardari* system which is the life of joint responsibility.

Quasi-proprietary rights.—Persons possessing quasi-proprietary rights are numerous. They may be classified according as their rights are or are not transferable :—

I.—Heritable and transferable—

Agra.—(*a*) Inferior proprietors where the settlement has been made with the superior proprietor.

(*b*) Permanent tenure-holders.

(*c*) Fixed-rate tenants.

Oudh.—(*d*) Sub-settlement-holders.

(*e*) Other under-proprietors.

II.—Heritable but not transferable—

Agra.—(*a*) Occupancy tenants.*

Oudh.—(*b*) Ditto.

(*c*) Permanent lessees.

(*d*) Tenants holding under special agreement or decree or given leases for the term of settlement in villages granted by Government.

TENANTS AND THE TENANCY LAWS.

Tenancy Legislation in Agra.—Act 10 of 1859 was passed for the protection of the tenants in Bengal and extended to the North-Western Provinces. It gave a

*The rights are transferable only by consent between persons in favour of whom as co-sharers in the tenancy such right originally arose, or who have become by succession co-sharers therein.

statutory right of occupancy to every tenant in respect of every field which he had occupied continuously for 12 years. After several amendments it was entirely remodelled in Act 12 of 1881, which, among other changes gave occupancy rights in their home farm (*sir*) to persons who parted with their proprietary rights (ex-proprietary tenants). The 12 years' rule however was left substantially unaltered. Increasing competition for land soon led landlords to obstruct the accrual of occupancy rights, which prevented the raising of rents. To prevent "continuous" holding which carried the right with it, the fields were shifted or the tenants nominally ejected every eleventh year or so. It became necessary to alter the law to meet the new situation and the result was the Tenancy Act of 1901. This enacts that continuity of holding is not interrupted by any shifting of the actual lands held, provided the holder is not left altogether without land for at least a year at a time. It is assumed that land to which a tenant is admitted by such shifting is given to him in exchange for his previous holding. Under the old Act, too, any period for which a tenant cultivated under a written lease could not be counted towards the 12 years necessary to acquire occupancy rights. The new Act provides that no written lease can bar the growth of occupancy rights unless it is for at least 7 years. Further, ejectment of ordinary tenants was made more difficult.

Tenancy legislation in Oudh.—No restrictive action was taken to prevent the rise of rents in Oudh for a decade after the restoration of order there. Under their *sanads* the taluqdars had to treat their tenants with consideration ; and they on the whole fulfilled their obligations. After the first regular settlement, however, rents were generally raised, and increasing competition for land began in southern Oudh. As the result of a special inquiry it was recommended that all tenants should be secured in their holdings for a period of 7 years, that the landlords should have power to eject after that term, but with a limit to the enhancement of rent in any new lease. These principles were accepted by the government, the limit of enhancement being fixed at $6\frac{1}{4}$ per cent. or 1 anna in the rupee and the result appears in the Oudh Rent Act of 1886, which is still in force, with minor amendments directed to permitting the creation of an occupancy right in their home farms in favour of ex-proprietors.

Special tenures in the permanently settled districts.—In the permanently settled districts of the province of Agra there are two special classes of tenants who have heritable and transferable interests and therefore a quasi-proprietary right. The two classes are known respectively as permanent tenure-holders and fixed-rate tenants. Both have held from the time of the permanent settlement without alteration in the rate of their rent and are entitled to continue to hold without change. The former class may be described as a kind of inferior proprietor, intermediate between the proprietor and the ordinary tenants, the others have technically a right of occupancy only, but they differ from ordinary occupancy tenants by possessing the right of transfer, unrestricted succession, and absolute fixity of rent.

Occupancy Tenants :—In Agra occupancy tenants have acquired their rights (i) by order of the settlement officer at the first regular settlement, between 1833 and 1849; (ii) as ex-proprietary tenants in the home farm; and (iii) by twelve years' continuous cultivation as defined in the Tenancy Act.

In Oudh, occupancy tenants have acquired their rights under the Oudh compromise, or the Oudh Laws Act, or the amending Rent Act of 1901; all are, in reality, exproprietary tenants, though their rights were acquired in different ways; some other tenants have been given occupancy rights in plots of land by decree of court, or agreement.

The value of an occupancy right is great. The holder of it cannot be ejected except for arrears of rent, and his rent can only be enhanced by written agreement, or by order of a revenue court, and then only under certain prescribed conditions. In Agra, the rents of occupancy tenants are not privileged, and are liable to enhancement at settlement and at intervals of 10 years; in Oudh, the rents of occupancy tenants are privileged to the extent of two annas in the rupee below those of statutory tenants. In both provinces ex-proprietary tenures are privileged to the extent of four annas in the rupee below the rate paid by non-occupancy tenants.